THE LAST SIX MINUTES

A Mother's Loss and Quest for Justice

"Written from the heart, to the heart, Sandra's book reveals the devastating and rippling effect of a violent crime from the most soul-rending perspective imaginable — that of a mother who's lost her child."

—Tom Zytaruk
Author & Journalist

"Sandra Martins-Toner is a warm, honest, and unassuming young woman. She has transcended the untimely death of her son by working to bring changes to the criminal justice system. Now she has written an account of her experience in the same way she speaks: openly, from her heart and soul."

—Wallace G. Craig - Retired Provincial Court Judge/Author

"Sandra's never-ending fight for justice is a battle we all have a critical stake in – her story rips the window dressing off the Canadian criminal justice system to reveal an institution awash in disgrace."

–John Martin: Criminologist, University of the Fraser Valley

"Having spent over twenty years as a trial lawyer, and close to twice as long immersed in the machinations of our political system, I know what energy and focus it takes to have any hope of effecting change to the "System". Sandra Martins-Toner, like Chuck Cadman before her, has channeled her grief into a constructive effort to improve the administration of justice in our country. Sandra's tireless work with FACT and, now, the willingness to detail her unimaginably painful experience in a book so as to benefit others is citizenship as it ought to be and moral courage of the highest order."

—David O. Marley, BA, LLB, MSc
Principal of BIAS 4 Action Public Affairs
Vancouver, BC

"This heart wrenching story is an inspiring "must read" for all the men and women of Law Enforcement, and those concerned with the escalating violent crimes plaguing our country. Families Against Crime & Trauma was forced into existence through lack of social accountability.

Judges no longer see themselves as serving the victims, and thousands of citizens are made victims by an apparently uncaring Criminal Justice System. Victims cry out for justice, only to find the 'justice' component has been removed. Judges have long abandoned/forgotten the reason they are there. Until they realize this, more of our children will be murdered, and the Sandra Martins-Toner's of our society have no other choice but to fight back. . .and I support them!"

—Len Miller, Detective (retired)
Vancouver Police Department

"As a mother, I am deeply touched by this very strong, courageous woman's fight for justice in the name of her son, Matthew. The fact that she is able to put into words her son's violent murder and her dealings with the Cimininal Justice System thereafter in such a remarkable book speaks volumes about the author. After crying through the first 58 pages, I got it together long enough to read the whole book and am left with a feeling of complete awe. Thank you for your never-ending fight for justice, Sandra!"

—Naomi Jones
Court Reporter

THE LAST SIX MINUTES

A Mother's Loss and Quest for Justice

SANDRA MARTINS-TONER

AASPIRATIONSPUBLISHING INC.

BUILDING COMMUNITIES THROUGH BOOKS

THE LAST SIX MINUTES A Mother's Loss and Quest for Justice

Copyright © 2009 by Sandra Martins-Toner.

Published by Aaspirations Publishing Inc.
www.aaspirationspublishing.com

Cover Photograph by Brian Howell
www.brianhowellphotography.com

Cover and Interior Book Design and Typesetting by Sue Balcer
www.JustYourType.biz

This book (except photographs) is printed on 100% post consumer recycled paper (ancient-forest-free, processed chlorine and acid free paper). It is in line with our policy of green publishing for which over 10,000 trees have been planted in collaboration with Ecolibris.net to help offset costs of production and transportation. For further information visit our website, www.aaspirationspublishing.com

Printed in Canada

First printing August 2009

ISBN 978-0-9812781-1-7

Copyright © 2009 by Sandra Martins-Toner. All rights reserved.

Aaspirations Publishing Inc.
Toronto   Delhi

Author's Note

Although this is a work of non-fiction, and the story of the tragic end of my young son's life, I have taken great care in omitting the names of the people who were witnesses to the crime, and those my son came into contact with that evening. This has enabled me to safely tell of the life and death of my child, and to remain true to what my family endured without putting anyone in danger or invading anyone's privacy.

The details of my family's life before, during and after the trial are my own, and I relied heavily upon notes, journal entries and my own memories in order to share the experience.

The portions of the book where I discuss the trial or any other legal proceedings can be found by any member of the public. All judgements are placed on the Supreme Court of British Columbia's website, and are matters of public record. I relied on these documents in order to write the statements made by the courts. I have also made sure that anything else I have disclosed has already been reported by the media, and is also available to the public.

I want to also inform anyone reading this book that the female convicted of second degree murder in our case had recently been granted an appeal, and has now been granted a second trial in the death of my son. We have been told that it could take many years to resolve, and that it is possible that her charges may be reduced, or she could be acquitted of her conviction, to walk a free woman. My family can only pray that we will not be dragged into years of court proceedings and the constant pain of having to listen to all of the horrific details of our young son's murder.

I have decided to write a sequel to this book regardless of the second trial's verdict. Should Katherine Quinn be absolved of her part in the killing of Matthew, we can rest knowing that Forslund will remain behind bars.

In writing this story, and sharing our personal tragedy, it is not my intention to demean any person(s) included. I have recounted the dialogue in this book to the best of my abilities and as truthfully as is humanly possible.

—Sandra Martins-Toner

Dedication

This book is dedicated to my beautiful son, Matthew Lee Martins, who has made me who I am today. I was a young mother, who, with all her heart, took full responsibility for bringing a child into her life. Matthew was the greatest gift: a wonderful, smart little boy, who would have one day become a great man. I am proud to have been blessed with this child, and will forever hold every moment, every laugh, and every memory close to my heart for the rest of my days. One day we will be together again. Some days that seems so far away that my heart fills with such terrible sadness and longing just to hold him once again. All I ask is to wake up from this terrible dream.

I also want to dedicate this book to my wonderful husband, David, who has been my strength, and the soft place I fall when I cannot bear the truth of it all. My wonderful sons, Mitchell and Braydan, who bring me so much joy and laughter, are also on the short list of those who have transformed me and sustained me. And I will not forget the sweetest little thing in my life, my daughter, Chhaya, who, through all the shock and pain of this loss, found her way into our lives when we needed her most.

There are no words to describe how one feels when you simultaneously lose a child and bring a child into the world. All I can say is she saved my life; she kept me from abusing myself during this nightmare which will forever circumscribe my life.

My three sisters, Jeane, Celia and Tina have been by my side through all of this; they have also suffered terribly. I love you all so very much; I thank God for all of you, every day of my life. Alone—we are nothing. You are my foundation—all that I am today, and all that I have become is because, individually and collectively, you were there to guide me, to help me along the way. Forever four, together strong.

I want to thank Nina Rivet, the co-founder of Families Against Crime & Trauma (F.A.C.T.) While writing this book, Nina left F.A.C.T. to pursue her other initiatives. To Nina, I would like to say, "You have helped me heal in ways I could never imagine. I never knew how strong one person could be until I met you."

This is for all the mothers who have lost a child, mother, father, brother or sister due to a violent crime. You are not alone, and you do not have to suffer alone.

If this book can help ease some pain, or just help another to understand that it is okay to feel what you are feeling, then I am satisfied; my work is done. I hope that Matthew's death will not have been in vain, but may provide a glimpse into the savage reality of today's world. We, as a society, must make changes to our justice system, so that our children's children will not have to live in fear. Those who are a danger should be dealt with swiftly and decisively.

To all the members and supporters of Families Against Crime & Trauma, (F.A.C.T.), who have allowed me to share my grief and pain, and who have stood alongside David and me in our fight for change, I extend my sincere gratitude.

I cannot forget my wonderful father, Louçiano, for being there for my sisters and me during the first few weeks of the trial. My father passed away suddenly just weeks before the end of the trial of Matthew's accused killers, but I know that he was looking down on all of us. I know you are with Matthew now, Daddy. You watch over him until I can get there.

Matthew Lee Martins—September 1988-July 2005
Until we are together again...

Acknowledgements

Besides those mentioned in the dedication,
I gratefully acknowledge the contributions of:

Wendy Dawson

Wallace G. Craig

Mary Ainslie

Cpl. David Teboul

Sgt. M. Mann

The I.H.I.T. Team

Gramma & Grampa

Gord & Kim Penner

Dan & Mark Sondheim

Brian Howell

Linda Urquhart

Paulette Hill

Moneca Melan

Claudette Sandecki

Cindy Vautour Smith

MLA Mike Farnworth

MLA Adrian Dix

F.A.C.T. Board of Directors

F.A.C.T. Members & Supporters

All those who have suffered loss due to a violent crime

TABLE OF CONTENTS

PREFACE xii

AUTHOR'S NOTE 5

ONE: THE NIGHTMARE UNFOLDS 1

TWO: HOW HE BEGAN – MATTHEW APPEARS 5

THREE: MATTHEW'S LAST EVENING 13

FOUR: THE HOSPITAL DRAMA CONTINUES 17

FIVE: MATTY'S GONE! 23

SIX: AFTERMATH AT HOME – PICKING UP THE PIECES 29

SEVEN: FUNERAL—EXPENSES AND EMOTION 37

EIGHT: AND LIFE GOES ON—IF THAT'S WHAT YOU CALL IT 45

NINE: THE ACCUSED SEEK BAIL 51

TEN: THE PROTESTS BEGIN—CRIMINAL JUSTICE ON TRIAL 57

ELEVEN: SKYTRAIN IMPROVEMENTS—ACTIVISM REWARDED 63

TWELVE: GUARDIAN ANGELS–COMMITMENT TO COMMUNITY 69

THIRTEEN: THE TRIAL BEGINS 73

FOURTEEN: THE TRIAL CONTINUES 79

FIFTEEN : THE LAST SIX MINUTES ON TAPE.............................85

SIXTEEN: KNIGHTS OF JUSTICE—THE HOMICIDE TEAM 89

SEVENTEEN: THE GANGSTA WANNA-BE.....................................95

EIGHTEEN: BABY ON BOARD—THE COURTROOM STAFF 101

NINETEEN: WITNESSES AND ACCUSED TESTIFY.................................105

TWENTY: ANOTHER LOSS...109

TWENTY-ONE: DREAMS: ATTORNEYS FOR THE DEFENCE 113

TWENTY-TWO: TOLL ON THE FAMILY: THERAPY.................................117

TWENTY-THREE: CLOSING ARGUMENTS 121

TWENTY-FOUR: THE JURY RETIRES; THE VERDICT 127

TWENTY- FIVE: PREPARING MY VICTIM IMPACT STATEMENT 133

TWENTY-SIX: MY TURN—ARTICULATING THE LOSS 141

TWENTY-SEVEN : SENTENCING AND JUDGE'S COMMENTS.............151

TWENTY-EIGHT: POST-TRIAL LIFE—F.A.C.T. IS BORN 157

TWENTY-NINE: CHANGING THE LAW IN BRITISH COLUMBIA...........161

THIRTY: A MOTHER'S MESSAGE TO HER SON'S KILLERS....................165

THIRTY-ON: THE GROUP SPAWNED BY MATT'S DEATH 171

EPILOGUE 175

DAVID TONER ON CANADIAN JURISPRUDENCE 175

APPENDIX 183

MATTHEW—IN HIS OWN VOICE 183

When a child loses his parents,
he is called an orphan.
When a spouse loses her or his partner,
he is called a widow or widower.

When parents lose their child,
there are no words to describe them.

~J. Neugeboren~

PREFACE

For two years I tried to write this book. I endured such pain in describing the details of my young son's murder, I realized that I needed more time to come to grips with it all. Every time I would picture the painful and horrific way in which Matthew's life had been taken, I just could not seem to get it out. It was too painful to relive, even in writing. I think it would be easier for me to just give the necessary details, thus sparing me the nightmares.

I have since had some time to cope with the pain, although it never really goes away. It just gets a little easier to remember all the good memories, rather than always thinking about Matthew's tragic end, and our final moments together.

Not only did I want to tell Matthew's story, but I felt it was important to address all the events that followed. People seem to think that we are able to just get over it, and move on with our lives. Honestly—nothing could be further from the truth. Not only does a parent lose a child or loved one, we often lose our jobs, our homes, our dignity, our peace of mind—and sometimes our mind itself. There is no greater shock to a parent's system. For families who have lost children and loved ones in this manner, there is never any closure. We never got to say goodbye, or even hold them as they took their final breath.

It has been just a little over three years since my sixteen-year-old son, Matthew, was taken from us. Some days it seems as though it has been forever since I have seen his beautiful face, or heard his angelic voice, and then there are moments where it seems to have just happened. It all rushes back as though I am re-living every moment, minute-by-minute, second-by-second. A true-life horror movie playing in slow motion, images and voices playing over and over in my head. The only difference is—I am not watching a horror movie, I am recalling in living—and dying—colour, my own life; there is no "off" switch.

When I decided to write about what had happened to Matthew, and our journey through the entire court/trial process, I was really doing it more for myself. It was a way to try to come to grips with everything I was feeling and going through. A cathartic process.

It was not until just recently, while I was in Seattle, Washington, that a simple gift from a wonderful man, Mr. Wallace Gilby Craig, made me realize I needed to share our story. We were panellists at a public discussion on crime at the Seattle Museum of History and Industry. He had brought a novel he wanted me to read—*Victims: the Orphans of Justice*, by Jerry Amernic.

This book tells the story of a family struggling to cope with the loss of their beautiful daughter, and the realization that the criminal justice system was solely concerned about the accused—not the victims or their families. It has been twenty-eight years since their loss and their fight. Regrettably, there has been little change in the way victims/families are treated.

Mr. Craig went on to say that he felt that our organization (Families Against Crime & Trauma—F.A.C.T.) needed to carry on where this book had left off.

For many years, victims/families who have lost a child or a loved one to a violent crime have been ignored, mute observers to the criminal justice system.

We not only endure the pain of our losses, but we are then discarded and tossed aside by the criminal justice system and the Canadian government. This story is about my family's fight to see Matthew's memory kept alive. It is also a testament to all the others who have joined us along the way in the hope of changing the criminal justice system, and the way victims/families are treated—before, during and after the trials.

Chapter One

THE NIGHTMARE UNFOLDS

These are the times that try men's souls.

~ Thomas Paine ~

*T*he telephone rang, piercing the stillness of our home in the wee hours of the morning. I remember hearing it, but I was not quite sure if I was dreaming or not. I do not have a phone in my bedroom, so I hurried down the hall to the kitchen to grab the closest one. I thought to myself, *Who could possibly be calling here at this ungodly hour?*— it was just after three a.m.

I actually thought that Matthew had already come home during the night; he always took great care to come in quietly, hoping not to rouse the two big dogs sleeping in the front of the house.

I kept thinking it was probably a wrong number, but I was wrong. When I picked up the receiver, I heard the voice of Matthew's close friend, the one he had been with that evening. He told me that Matthew had been assaulted, and that he was calling me from the back of a police car, as the officers wanted to question him. None of what he said made sense, of course, and I began to shout at him, asking him where Matthew was, how this had happened. He had no answers for me. All he could say was he had overheard the officers saying Matthew had been taken to Royal Columbian Hospital.

I hung up the phone, ran to my bedroom and told David what I had just heard. I quickly grabbed the white pages, still not even sure what I was supposed to be looking for. In my stupor I leafed through it to the Hospital pages, ripping half the pages as I went along. I dialled the emergency ward number that was listed for the hospital, and the phone rang for what seemed an eternity. The voice on the other end patched me through to the emergency department, and they confirmed that a young male had been recently admitted as a "John Doe," someone without any identification.

I told the nurse that I suspected it might be my son, and began to give her a description. The nurse stated that it sounded like a match, but that we should come in to confirm. I told her that we were on our way, and was told not to hurry—there was no rush.

The drive to New Westminster never seemed so long. We drove quickly, but not crazily, trying to think positively, as all parents must at a point like that. I kept thinking that he was probably banged up, maybe needed stitches. I tried to interpret what the nurse had said—that there was no need to rush. Nothing could have prepared me for what followed.

Upon arrival at Royal Columbian Hospital, we identified ourselves to the nurse at the emergency desk, and after she spoke to someone on the phone, we were directed into a small room off the waiting area. It seemed strange, as the general waiting room was not that crowded. It was still so early in the morning.

After just a short wait, another nurse appeared and introduced herself. She told us that the medical staff believed, based on our description of him, that they had Matthew in the emergency ward. He had been assaulted and was unconscious. However, as there was no ID on him, they needed someone to confirm it was really him.

My husband explained that I was pregnant, and that he thought he would be better able to go, given my state. The nurse led David down the corridor to a trauma room where several nurses and doctors were busy working on a prone form on a stretcher. My husband later told me that, at that point, the nurse escorting him grabbed him firmly by the upper arm, perhaps fearing he might collapse at the sight. David approached the boy on the gurney as the doctors and nurses, as if by some silent cue, backed away and allowed him room to stand at the bedside. All stood quietly while David looked at the face of the young man on the stretcher. My husband was taken aback. Along with the usual blood, abrasions and bruising that is common to any violent altercation, he was also surprised by the amount of swelling in the face. He had to look carefully, recognizing his stepson not as one usually would with a casual glance, but by purposefully scanning for a familiar mole, and finally recognizing the camouflage boxer shorts Matt was always wearing around the house. It was Matt, and he was in bad shape.

They led David back into the waiting room where I had been rocking myself back and forth on a cold vinyl couch, praying that Matthew would be okay. The nurse was clutching David's upper arm as she led him back into the room. David was pale, and looked like he had just witnessed something he would take to the grave with him. I had never seen that look on my husband's face before.

I knew something was wrong—very wrong. David looked at me, looked away, and then back again before saying, "It's Matty, but I had a hard time recognizing him."

The police officers in the room with us asked us all sorts of questions. They wanted to know who Matthew had been with that night, what time he had left the house, everything and anything to help them put together a timeline of the evening's events.

David and I answered all the questions as thoroughly as possible in hopes of helping them. They told us that they had two people in custody, and that they were certain they were the ones who had assaulted Matthew. At the time, that was all they could tell us, but they promised they would keep us informed.

Doctors soon joined us in the room—the walls now seemed to be closing in on us. I couldn't breathe, couldn't think—my normal world was falling apart right before my eyes; I could do nothing to stop it.

4

Chapter Two

HOW HE BEGAN – MATTHEW APPEARS

A babe in the house is a well-spring of pleasure,
a messenger of peace and love,
a resting place for innocence on earth,
a link between angels and men.

~ Martin Farquhar Tupper ~

*I*n the fall of 1987, while most young girls my age were out scouring the malls for the ultimate prom dress, I could be found fretfully rummaging through the clearance racks of Zellers for oversized t-shirts and sweatpants. I couldn't help but feel doubly miserable as I walked through the mall, looking through the storefront windows at the beautiful gowns my girlfriends would wear to prom. Watching these girls, most of them my schoolmates, run from store to store with their mothers and giggly girlfriends in tow, was agonizing. I wanted nothing more than to be able to wear a beautiful gown with crystals and beads adorning the bodice and sleeves, but there was no way I would be able to fit into any off-the-rack gowns. I had a growing tummy. As Shakespeare put it, I was "big with child."

At sixteen, I found myself in a situation every teen (and parent of teen) dreads: I was pregnant. I never thought it would happen to me; I had never felt so alone in my life. I was pregnant and scared. I wasn't sure how much longer I could hide the truth from my parents. I think they attributed my sudden weight gain to puberty and stress, but little did they know where the stress emanated from; I was already into the second trimester of my pregnancy.

Academically, I had proven I was a smart young girl, but unfortunately, my intelligence did not transfer over to street smarts. I had been raised in a very old-fashioned home with parents who never spoke to their children about sex, drugs or even puberty. Had I not been the youngest of four girls, I would have been completely clueless. My parents, both landed immigrants from Portugal, shielded my sisters and me from the outside world. I don't think they intended to raise us in ignorance. They just didn't know any better.

This was how they had been raised, and it was how they raised my sisters and me. Sexual topics were taboo; things you would never discuss with your mother or father.

I remember the day I told my mother that I was pregnant. All she could say to me was that I was going to kill my father with this news. My heart broke at the thought of my father being disappointed in me. I had always had a wonderful relationship with my father—I was the epitome of a "Daddy's girl." My father had always wanted a son, but after having four girls, they decided to call it quits, and just be thankful for the blessings they had. Dad was happy enough to have me as his little shadow, following him everywhere he went, including to work.

Our relationship never faltered—I worshipped the ground my father walked on. In my eyes, there was no man on this earth who could ever compare to my Daddy. Although we were sheltered, we were, nonetheless, happy young girls who grew up in a home filled with laughter, love and a genuine sense of family.

To hear my mother say that I was going to disappoint him was beyond devastating. I begged my mother to allow me some time to find a way to tell him, but eventually my mother just blurted it out as we all sat in our living room together.

It took my father a moment to absorb what my mother had just announced. He looked from my mother to me, over and over, until he realized what he had just been told.

I was furious with my mother for telling, but understood that time was running out. My tiny frame could no longer hide the growing bump I had been trying so hard to keep hidden. For the duration of my pregnancy my father scarcely looked in my direction, let alone spoke to me.

I was devastated by his silence, and cried myself to sleep many nights, wishing he would say something—anything—to ease my mind.

I continued to attend school, but was transferred to another program for teenage mothers, so I could finish my courses even after I had the baby. As my tummy began to get bigger and bigger, I felt the need to try and reach out to the baby's father. I needed him to know that I was pregnant, just in case he wanted to try and have a relationship with the child. My parents were furious with my decision, but I wanted to do it.

I had just turned seventeen when I gave birth to a perfect, seven-pound, three-ounce baby boy. I named him Matthew Lee Martins. He was born on September 20, 1988, in Burnaby, British Columbia, a suburb of Vancouver.

He was an angel from the moment he came into my life. The second I realized I was pregnant, I knew that I was going to do whatever it took to have my baby, and raise it the best I could. I had Matthew in September, and immediately returned to school at the end of October in order to graduate with my peers.

I was very thankful that once Matthew was born, my father came around and began to speak to me again. He was in love with this beautiful little boy, his second grandchild, and he did all he could to help in raising him.

I still remember hearing my father quietly entering my bedroom in the middle of the night to check on the baby. His little crib was tucked in next to my single bed, so that I could reach over to him should he awake in the night. I watched my father standing there, peering into his crib, pulling up his little blankets, gently stroking the side of Matthew's tiny little head.

My sister Jeane had also had a son just four years before me, but the situation was a little different. My sister had already been living abroad and on her own when she had my nephew, Danny. Jeane and Danny returned to Canada when her son was nine months old, and we all resided in the same home, under our parents' roof. Danny and Matthew grew up more like brothers than cousins. Through the years, they became inseparable; Matthew was always trying to keep up with Danny, idolizing him as they grew older.

Matthew was an exceptionally gifted child. An amazingly bright and talented little boy, he spoke very well even before he turned two. His love for music was apparent at the same early age. I remember vividly how he made me play music for him so he could fall asleep. The artists varied from one night to the other, but one thing always remained the same—the music had to be played until he was fast asleep. Matthew's ability to learn the lyrics to songs by the age of four was astounding. He could recall the name of a song and the band that performed it, just by listening to me hum a few bars.

This child sang from the moment he woke up until it was time for bed. My sisters and I always asked him to sing to us at family functions, as we were in awe of his beautiful, sweet voice. I still remember that shortly after Matthew passed away, one of my neighbours mentioned that they always knew when Matthew was arriving home, because they could hear him singing all the way down the block.

I married Matthew's father in 1991, and went on to have two more beautiful little boys, each exactly four years apart. However, this marriage was doomed from the beginning and by the time Matthew was nine years old, I left with the boys to begin our new lives.

I eventually met my husband, David, in 1998, and we married in 2001. I felt blessed to have met a man who loved my boys as much as he loved me. I had actually resigned myself to accepting that I was going to be a single mother of three for the rest of my life. After all, who would want to involve themselves in a ready-made family, with all the baggage that it entailed?

It was not long after we met that Matthew, on his own accord, began to call David, "Dad," and soon his younger brothers followed suit. Braydan had been just a toddler learning to walk when we first met, so in his life there had been no other father.

Matthew came to love being in the spotlight, and as he grew he would take great pride in performing for anyone willing to watch and listen. His charisma and charm always drew others to him.

Matthew and I not only had a relationship as mother and son, but as best friends. We grew up together, learning so much from one another over the years. I can remember many occasions when we had been asked if we were siblings. One time, during a seventh grade parent-teacher meeting, I arrived at the classroom only to be asked if Matty's mother was going to be able to attend the meeting as well. We looked at each other and laughed.

My son always had a soft spot for the underdog. He made a point to always support those who needed it most. He had struggled most of his life with the fact that he was always the smallest, the one who couldn't run the fastest, who was left-handed in a right-handed world. He felt he was always the odd man out. He was bullied terribly in elementary school by the bigger kids, yet he always found a way to rise above the hurt, and came to grips with the fact that he could not change how others perceived him.

Once Matthew became a teen, he really began to shine. It was music that would evaporate his insecurities. He began performing for our local Boys & Girls Club for the younger kids, becoming a mentor for the little ones. It didn't matter where we were in our community, the kids always ran up to him to say hi, and to ask when he was coming back to teach them how to breakdance or free style.

He was also a great friend to his peers. His ability to listen and never judge, made him a very true and special friend. Watching my son overcome so much strife in his life taught me as a mother to never give up. The lessons I learned from him will remain with me forever.

Matty would tell us on a daily basis that one day he was going to be famous, but never in a million years did I ever think that my son's face would grace the covers of newspapers and magazines because of his tragic end.

I chose to share Matthew's life and death because I needed a way to keep my son's memory alive, and I wanted to be able to reach out to other parents and families who have lost their loved ones to violent crimes. Once the trials are over, the juries have made their decisions, and the media on the steps has dispersed, the families are left alone and often isolated. The hole left in the hearts of the families of murder victims does not go away.

To every family, the death of a loved one is very sad and traumatic. But the circumstances that present themselves when

11

a member has been murdered can cause a multitude of different emotions, and stresses that no one could be prepared for.

Families of murder victims are forced to deal with the overwhelming grieving process as well as the trauma of the judicial process. Their sense of living in a fair and just world is shattered. Those who are left behind, trying to pick up the pieces, find it next to impossible to make any sense of the heinous crime.

I want people to not only remember my son as he lived, but to also remember the senseless, random, violent act that took his life.

Matthew's life was snuffed out just two months before he would have turned seventeen. It was almost exactly my age when I had given birth to him.

I want to share with you not just the pain of our loss, but the journey into healing from the most horrific days of our lives. I hope to help others who may find themselves standing in my shoes. Some details of what happened that night will never be known, as the perpetrator has not divulged; the truth died with Matthew.

Chapter Three

MATTHEW'S LAST EVENING

The deepest definition of youth is life as yet untouched by tragedy.

~ Alfred North Whitehead ~

On July 1st, 2005, Matthew and his friends were deciding what they should do to celebrate the Canada Day festivities. That day began no differently than any other. We went through the motions with nothing out of the ordinary.

Matthew spent the early part of his afternoon over at his good friend's house, visiting. He arrived home shortly before dinner. He listened to his music in his room before venturing out to see what was happening for dinner.

My husband David and I had gone out to fetch the kids some pizza, as I was eight weeks pregnant at the time and just the thought of cooking made me ill. As David and I drove home with the pizza, I decided that I wanted Chinese take-out instead, so we decided to drop the pizza off with the boys, and go out again to satisfy my Chinese food craving.

The boys sat together arguing over how many slices of the pizza each would get. This is a pizza ritual in our house—they all have to have the same, exact amount, or a fight erupts. The boys are exactly four years apart, and they have never had a problem finding something to argue over. It could be a TV show one wants to watch, or even a game they can't decide on playing at the same time. So, like most days, there was nothing to suggest today would be any different than any other day.

While David and I were out, Matthew received a phone call from a friend who resides in a neighbouring suburb, Surrey, B.C. Matthew was invited to attend the fireworks being held in Cloverdale (in Surrey). Matty agreed to meet with his friends. He finished his dinner with his brothers and informed Mitchell, our middle son, of his plans for the night.

Matthew had already left when I arrived home with my Chinese food. I live with that terrible guilt every day of my life. *Why did I have to want Chinese food, why couldn't I have just been happy with pizza that day?*

I think I would have told him that I didn't want him to go out to Surrey. Actually—I know I would have forbidden him to go.

When Matthew and his friends arrived at the fireworks site, people were being evacuated—some sort of propane or gas leak had occurred. The crowds dispersed; the boys began their trek back to the local friend's home.

At some point during the night, Matthew was called by a female friend who asked him if he could meet her close to the Surrey Central SkyTrain Station. It was while he walked alone to meet his friend, that Katherine Quinn, twenty-two, her boyfriend, Robert Forslund, twenty-seven, and a few of their friends partying outside of their home noticed Matty walking towards them.

According to testimony and statements, Quinn made a comment to a friend standing next to her about Matthew's chain and crucifix. As he proceeded to walk past them, Quinn jumped him from behind, pulling at his necklace.

This would be the beginning of the end for my little boy. During the scuffle, Quinn and Matthew fell onto the road. Somehow, Quinn was scratched with something. She began screaming to her friends and to her boyfriend, Forslund, that she had been stabbed. Matthew got up and began to run—in hopes of getting away from the attackers—but they chased him to the station and cornered him at the bottom of the escalators. Some gave chase on foot, while the others used their car to pursue him. Once they found him, they robbed him and beat him so severely that he was unrecognizable to his own mother and father. Matthew was thrown head first into the Plexiglas bus shelters not once, but three times. His head was stomped on over thirty times, squashed and shattered like a pumpkin. They not only beat him, but then proceeded to use a broken beer bottle to slit his throat.

The Integrated Homicide Investigation Team, (I.H.I.T.) officers later seized pieces of beer bottle from the crime scene which matched the fragments of glass the pathologist later found in Matthew's mouth, and in his esophagus. The pathologist's opinion was that the glass fragments had been swallowed, or that it was also possible the fragments could have been pushed from Matthew's mouth into his esophagus during medical intervention. The paramedics described seeing broken glass all around Matthew and in his body as well. Matty had nearly bled out at the foot of the escalators by the time the paramedics could reach him. The paramedics noted that Matthew had a long gaping cut on the right side of his neck, amongst all the other injuries to his head and body.

Once he was taken to the hospital, the operating surgeon described the wound as being eight centimetres in length. The emergency room doctor also described the laceration, stating that the cut to Matthew's neck had not cut any major blood vessels—it was not the cause of his death. The autopsy later revealed that Matthew had sustained multiple abrasions to his body, and that there were thirty-eight points of impact trauma to his head and neck area. The blows and stomps to his head ended his life.

Our saving grace was that the entire assault was caught on the surveillance cameras in the station. Otherwise, it was unlikely that my son's killers would ever have been charged and convicted of second degree murder. This was the last six minutes of my child's life—all caught on video.

Chapter Four
THE HOSPITAL DRAMA CONTINUES

We all live in a house on fire,
no fire department to call; no way out,
just the upstairs window to look out of
while the fire burns the house down
with us trapped, locked in it.

~ Tennessee Williams ~

*T*he doctors were not giving us much information on Matthew's condition or about what they were doing. They told us that he was in critical condition; he had received a blood transfusion due to severe blood loss. At that point, all I knew was that he had been assaulted, and the beating had been severe.

We sat in the waiting room for what seemed like forever. I remember asking David to call my sisters and ask them to come to the hospital, although I vaguely remember him calling my sister, Celia, before we left the house. If she were to give you her version of that phone call, she would tell you that she was so angry with David—she didn't understand what he was telling her in his mad rush to get us to the hospital. The call would play in her head over and over again, until the cold reality started to sink in.

Once David returned from making the calls, we were asked to move to another room on one of the upper floors of the hospital. I realize now they moved us into an area for those who were awaiting their loved ones' last hours. It was a place where families could say their final goodbyes. Just thinking about it makes me a little uneasy. The room was small; two couches, one in front of the other, a window facing another building across the way, a table with a phone to call others for support and bulletins. I tried to lie down while we waited for my sisters and family to arrive, but nothing could stop the thoughts running through my brain.

I was beginning to sweat profusely; nausea had begun to overwhelm me. I asked a nurse for some ice water, in hopes that it would help alleviate the discomfort. Every second we waited for news felt like an eternity.

My family began arriving; the look of panic in their eyes was hard to shake off. We all sat huddled, waiting, praying for someone to come and tell us that Matthew was going to be okay, but that did not happen.

We were finally told that Matthew was going to be taken for an MRI of his brain to see how much damage there was. The news gave me a glimmer of hope, but it was soon dashed by the look on the doctor's face. I have worked long enough alongside many doctors to know that look: a look of absolute defeat. I knew instantly that they had exhausted every means known to them, but could not find a way to save this child, my beautiful child.

I remember asking the doctor to call the local parish to have a priest come and sit with us to pray for Matthew. Father Michael arrived within the hour, and I begged him to help us pray, and to ask God to spare my child. We all sat, heads bowed, tears streaming, praying together in unison. I was on my knees, clutching Father Michael's legs, begging him to pray harder, to say anything that would help my son survive this beating. He just looked into my eyes with his kind face and said nothing. What could he say? He could not promise me anything; he could not change the sequence of events that were soon to follow.

Eventually, two doctors entered the room; a man and a woman this time. I remember trying to search their eyes for any clues, but was struck by the oddity of the female doctor. She wore her white lab coat, and had on a beaded necklace that seemed quite large. I found it strange as I couldn't imagine how she could work with trauma patients wearing such bulky jewellery. Don't ask me why I was thinking that—I just was. Perhaps in my own way I welcomed any distraction from the inevitable. David later told me that he also noted the apparent youth of the female surgeon. He didn't think she looked old enough to be a doctor, let alone a surgeon.

I was still kneeling on the floor holding on to Father Michael's knees, as he sat across from me on the couch. The doctors sat down across from me. David was sitting on the couch behind me.

The Last Six Minutes

I honestly can't remember who else was in the room at the time, but I think that my sisters had just arrived as the male doctor began to speak to us.

As he began to speak, I had an out-of-body experience; I felt as though I were outside my body, watching the scene unravel like a movie. His words floated out of him, in slow motion. He stated that they had done the MRI on Matthew's brain.

It was not good. He felt that Matthew would not survive the severe beating. I tried to put it all into perspective, like piecing a puzzle together. It wasn't until they told me that Matthew was completely brain dead—he was being kept alive by machines—that I realized the absolute finality of it all. They were going to keep monitoring his vitals, but felt at this time we should say our goodbyes.

My body felt heavy—I could not even move. I screamed and screamed, wanting it to be a bad dream. I begged them to save my son, and began clutching and grabbing at everyone.

The female doctor had tears streaming down her face. She was at a loss as to what to say or do. David cradled me on the floor. My sisters were now falling apart at what they had just heard. We could not come to grips with this horrific news, but all I wanted was to be with Matthew, to hold his tiny little body in my arms and rock him like I did when he was a baby. Where was he? Why wasn't I allowed to be by his side? Just as those thoughts ran through my mind, I heard the sound of sneakers pounding and screeching across the hospital floors outside the room. The beeping and chiming sounds of the machines were coming closer and closer. It was Matthew, on a stretcher. He was being pushed quickly from one end of the hospital to another. I could see them hurrying past us, but as I tried to dart out the door to Matthew, I was stopped by the Victim's Services worker who had been sitting outside the room in case she was needed. Why was she keeping me from him? I wanted to push her out of my way, but was held back by my husband.

I asked the male doctor who was now standing in the doorway trying to keep us calm, to please allow Father Michael to be with Matthew if we could not. I begged him to baptize Matthew, and pray for him at his bedside and give him extreme unction. Father Michael asked if the baptism would be what Matthew wanted, and I assured him that Matthew never went a day without his crucifix; he had had a great faith in God since early childhood. I needed this more than anything. I needed to know that he would be blessed if he was about to leave this world and make his journey to heaven.

My family was eventually allowed into the ICU to be at Matthew's side. We surrounded his bed, taking turns holding his hands. His body was draped in sheets and towels, with only his hands and feet uncovered, to prevent us from seeing the extent of the damage. But, as we sat watching over him, blood could be seen seeping slowly through the towels around his head and neck. At regular intervals, nurses would usher us out of the room to change the towels, and then let us back in.

Looking back at those last hours at the hospital, I am struck by the gaps in my memory. I can only surmise that I was hysterical and out of it. And then there were periods of perfect clarity, where

The Last Six Minutes

I remember the smallest detail. I recall the coppery smell of his blood in the air, and the nausea that accompanied it. I remember my cousin, Jose, suddenly being there, although I cannot recall who notified him. I was talking out loud, talking to Matthew and about him.

I screamed out, "Why did they kill my baby?" Jose sharply reminded me in Portuguese that Matthew was not yet dead, perhaps trying to give me hope that there could be another outcome.

I told Matthew how much I loved him, and how proud we all were of him. I continued to ask why, over and over, why this had happened, how this could have happened. I held his hands, the only part of him that I could hold, and kissed his fingers. They were cold, limp and unresponsive to my touch. I could not believe that this was the child who, just earlier that day, had been walking around our home, singing and laughing.

Chapter Five
MATTY'S GONE!

God's finger touched him and he slept.

~ Lord Alfred Tennyson ~

*A*t approximately 8:30 in the morning, a nurse came in and advised us of his status. There was no brain activity, Matthew's vitals were not improving, and we had to make a decision. He was being kept alive by the machines, and we all knew that wasn't what Matthew would have wanted. I sat in a chair at his side, trying to grasp everything we were being told. I had so many questions about what we were about to do, but no answers. My cousin Rose stood behind my chair, wiping my face and neck with a cold cloth as I cried hysterically. I knew now what was about to happen, and what I was about to lose. I was being asked to turn off the machines that were breathing for him, and the thought of doing so was excruciating.

The Last Six Minutes

My sisters and I hugged one another, and with no words exchanged, we were able to make the decision to allow Matthew to go. I carefully placed my head on Matthew's pillow and told him that I was not going to be selfish by keeping him hooked up to these machines. I told him how much I loved him, and how we would soon be together again. At this time one, of my family members went to the nurse's station to advise them that we had come to a decision, and would like them to come and explain what was going to happen next. My sister Celia collapsed to the floor from the shock, and I could do nothing to move myself away from Matthew to help her. David and the others quickly lifted her tiny body from the ground and held her as she sobbed uncontrollably.

The nurse told us that they would turn the machine off when we were ready, and that Matthew needed to try to breathe for himself. I asked the nurse if it was going to be painful for him. She assured me that it was not, as there was no brain activity, and that he would be unaware of any pain. I also remember asking her how long he could survive breathing on his own, and to this she replied that for everyone it is different.

I don't remember how long we stood there before we looked at one another, and then looked over to the nurse, waiting for our signal to turn off the machine. I placed my head on Matthew's chest, looking under the edge of the towel covering his face to see his beautiful mouth. I told him to soar through the clouds, and fly free. I cried uncontrollably as I felt his lungs take in one last breath on his own, before his chest remained still.

There are no words to describe what I was feeling. The pain so incredibly physical, I thought I was about to die. I wanted to die; I wanted it to be me lying there at that very moment. There was nothing for me to live for, if I couldn't have my little boy with me. I couldn't believe it had ended so quickly for him, on the edge between boy and man. I couldn't comprehend the thought that this was going to be the last time I was going to be near Matthew.

I was going into shock and my brain was on overload. I became numb immediately and I retreated into a dark corner of my brain to hide from the pain. My spirit shattered into a million pieces, and a big part of me was gone forever.

I cursed the God who could have allowed this to happen. My faith completely ripped off its foundation. I never believed the God I had worshipped all my life could permit such an innocent to meet such an end. I felt a surge of anger pulse through me, almost as though I had been betrayed by Jesus himself.

It took a very long time before I prayed again without being angry. It was a while before I could resuscitate my faith, which I kept hidden in the dark crevices of my heart.

Matthew passed away on July 2, 2005 at 9:45 in the morning, six-and-a-half hours after being admitted. His tiny body could not fight the tremendous damage he had sustained from the beating.

We sat with Matthew's body for a while, even after the nurse had pronounced his time of death. David lifted my limp body from the chair and began to guide me down the long corridor leading out of the room. I remember looking back over my shoulder at Matthew a

25

few times as we walked away, and the sense of abandonment hit me like a ton of bricks. How could I leave my baby behind in this place? Would his soul wander these hallways looking for me? Would he try to find his way home to me ever again? My mind filled with terrible dread as we left the room. My cousins Jose and Dave remained with Matthew even after we left the room, and to this day I have never asked them why they had stayed behind. I think they needed a moment without me there to fall apart, as they had tried to remain stoic and brave in my presence.

Once the double doors opened to the main corridor of that floor, I was approached by a woman, the same woman from Victim Services. She produced some booklets and handed them to me, saying they would help me understand the process of grieving. I remember looking at her for a few moments, wondering what the hell she was talking about. Was it possible there were instructions on how I was supposed to feel and cope? I thought her "assistance" was ludicrous, and I felt like smacking her over the head with the booklets she had just handed me. What kind of a crazy person would hand you this sort of thing moments after your child has died?

I said nothing. I just looked at David and told him I wanted to retrieve Matthew's belongings before we went home. As soon as I said the words 'go home', my chest tightened at the thought that I now had to go home and tell Matthew's two younger brothers that their big brother had died.

We were told to go to the emergency ward to pick up Matthew's belongings, so my cousin Rose sat me down and went to speak to the nurses about Matthew's things. Rose was only gone a few minutes before she returned empty-handed. The nurses had told her that the police officers had taken his clothing for evidence and anything else Matthew might have had on him had probably been stolen during the robbery. I was so numb by this point, that I was nothing more than a moving corpse, a dead mother. I had to leave the hospital with nothing—not a single personal item from his last day to remember my beautiful Matthew.

Chapter Six

AFTERMATH AT HOME – PICKING UP THE PIECES

A faith that hasn't been tested can't be trusted.

~ Adrian Rogers ~

*T*he days that followed Matthew's death can only be described as horrific. Our home filled with friends and family trying to help us with the boys and the housework, and any other things they could find to do around our home. It seemed Matthew's murder was on every news channel, and headlined in all the local papers, even days after it happened. David and I spoke to the media very openly in hopes of creating awareness, and because we wanted the world to know that his life had been stolen for nothing more than a necklace and crucifix.

As painful as it was to invite the millions of viewers into our lives, at the darkest point in our lives, it seemed the right thing to do. We knew immediately that we would not allow the responsible parties who had murdered our son to get away with it.

Matthew's death was referred to in the media as the SkyTrain Murder, and the site began to draw people. A makeshift memorial sprang up at the spot where he fell, with family members, friends and strangers alike leaving flowers and candles. Camera crews hovered around, getting public reaction to the crime and for as long as two weeks after the murder, the little memorial stayed in place. Translink officials maintained that Matthew's death was not a reflection of the security situation at SkyTrain Stations, yet left the memorial and those coming to view it, undisturbed.

The doorbell rang continuously with floral deliveries from across Canada, from our friends and family. Food arrived hourly and there was no space left available in our kitchen or dining room to store any more food. The flowers arrived by the van-load and took over the entire house. We had to begin placing them along the stairs outside, leading to the entrance of our home. I know the gifts were sent out of kindness and sympathy, but it was all just too much.

I was getting extremely nauseated from all the different smells, and the strong perfume of the lilies. I spent the next few days doing nothing more than vomiting, sipping ice water, and trying to be gracious to all those who arrived at our home. I am sure much of my illness had to do with the pregnancy, but the stress and shock was not helping the situation.

My younger sons, Braydan and Mitchell, retreated to their rooms and scarcely spoke to anyone. They saw how much pain I was in, making them afraid to speak to me about anything they were feeling. I was even ignoring their questions about what had happened to their brother. I didn't know how to tell them about what had happened to Matthew, and I was afraid of how they would react to the viciousness of the crime. I could hear them screaming and crying in their rooms, but I could barely get myself to move from the bed or couch to console them. I didn't know what to say or do to help them, as I could not even help myself. David had to be the one to comfort them and hold them for the first week or so. Braydan began to sleep in our room at night, as he was terrified to be on his own. We fell asleep in each other's arms, exhausted from crying throughout the day. Sleep only came through sheer exhaustion, and even then it was a very broken sleep. I would wake in the middle of the night and pace through the house in the dark, only to return to the chaise lounge in front of the bay window, watching and waiting for Matthew to come home. I spent the next several months waiting for hours throughout the day and night. I began to convince myself that Matthew was not dead, that he was just away on holiday somewhere, and he would be coming home very soon. I was getting sick, and falling into a terrible depression by willing these thoughts to come true. I was not only in danger of losing my mind, but soon I became very aware that the baby in my womb was suffering terribly as well.

We got a call around the 5th of July that Matthew's body was ready to be released from the hospital, and they needed to know where to take him for his funeral arrangements. We had already decided that Matthew should be buried in the same cemetery as our grandparents, in Burnaby, B.C.. We were also waiting for my nephew Danny to return from Portugal where he had been visiting with our father for the past year. I could not bury Matthew without his cousin Danny there to say his final goodbyes to the only brother he had ever known.

On a July morning that seemed far too bright and sunny in contrast to the sombre purpose of our visit, we arrived at Forest Lawn Funeral Home, along with my aunt and her sons, Jose and Dave. We had no idea what needed to be done, what costs to expect—or anything else.

The funeral director we dealt with was younger than I had expected, but very professional and compassionate. He explained the things that needed to be done, and helped us with the questions we had. I remember asking him if Matthew was there, and he replied that he was; he had arrived that morning.

We were led down the hall to another room to view the coffins, and it seemed in a very surreal way like the showroom at any large car dealership. The caskets were on display; everything from the basic model that was little more than a cardboard box with cloth covering, to monstrous mahogany and metal pieces that resembled works of art. The former, we were told, were used mostly for cremations. As a Catholic, I wanted my son buried in a dignified way, and we eventually chose a casket that was neither flashy nor unduly simple. I liked the little cherubs that sat on each corner, somehow befitting a child, and there was a small drawer inside that could be filled with special belongings to be buried with Matthew. In this drawer I placed his iPod, some family photos, a rosary, and a letter written by his cousins. These things would accompany him on his journey.

David and I were both surprised at the costs of the casket, burial, and the funeral services. Having never been directly involved in anyone's funeral before, we were shocked at how much everything cost. We had no idea this was just the beginning of the tallies, and by the end of the day we would be panic-stricken, wondering how we were going to afford to bury our son.

Once we had decided on the casket and the service details with the funeral director, he drove us to another office to begin preparing to arrange for the purchase of a plot for Matthew's burial. This was the most traumatic and degrading part of the process for me. I remember following a young woman down a corridor to a room that would send me into an absolute anxiety attack. As she walked in through a doorway to her left, leading us into the room, I was hit immediately by the floor to ceiling grave markers and bronze panels all bearing the name "MATTHEWS." I could not even enter the room and was caught by my cousin Dave as I stumbled away from the door. I hid my face in his chest and sobbed uncontrollably, and the young woman couldn't figure out what had just happened.

Dave told her that my son's name was Matthew, and that the sight of his name on every single marker was just too much to deal with. My cousin whispered softly to me that I need not worry—it was not Matthew, but the name of the manufacturer. He did what he could to calm my nerves.

I realized that I needed to do this. However, I wanted nothing more than to be out of the place, so I kept my eyes averted to the floor in order to remain calm.

We looked through catalogues to choose a face plate and marker. We again had the distinct feeling that we were purchasing a product, that this was just another source of revenue for a business enterprise. It hit me that the person helping us was, first and foremost, a salesperson.

We were again loaded into a van to tour the cemetery and choose a resting place. I should point out here that we had no idea that a burial plot was real estate. We were about to find out how true that is. I asked to see some plots close to the area my grandparents were buried, only to be told this part of the cemetery was called a "heritage area" and prices started at eighteen thousand dollars. My knees buckled; tears streamed down my face, searing the cold flesh of my cheeks. We looked at each other and realized there was just no way we could afford that price. I think I said something inappropriate about commissions. We asked if there was something more reasonable available. The saleswoman responded in what we felt was a very callous fashion, saying that if we wanted to look at something "low end", she had some spots near the street.

I looked over to where she was pointing and I felt as though my heart had just been pulled out of my chest. This could not be happening, I was not about to place my baby up against the fence, and close to the main road. I would have sold my soul to the highest bidder at that very moment, in order to bury my son in a beautiful spot. David and my cousins glared at her, and she backtracked quickly, saying she had some nice spots up on the hill near the mausoleum. The spot on top of the hill was nice, and I liked it immediately. It faced south and had a view overlooking the rest of the cemetery. However, the cost was still high, at twelve thousand dollars. I held David and cried, still at a loss as to how we could come up with this money. We had no life insurance on our kids, never once thinking that we would outlive them. My wonderful cousins, seeing our distress, told us they would help out, and that they would make it happen.

We returned to the office to sign some papers, and set the date of the funeral for July 15, 2005. With the funeral services, the plot and interment, the total cost of Matthew's funeral was to be over twenty-seven thousand dollars. This, of course, was without any of the frills sometimes associated with memorial services, such as memorial cards, a spray of flowers for the casket, and flowers for the church. A few of our family friends bought the flowers for the church as a gift to Matthew, and my cousins made the most beautiful memorial cards on their own home computers, with Matthew's picture and a poem, to give out at the service.

My husband and I returned home that day, feeling spent and desperate. We now had to find the funds for the burial. We discovered how generous and compassionate people can be. David's employer donated money. Each of our family members who were able, put in what they could afford. My sister started a trust fund, and our media contacts helped out, announcing the details on the news coverage of the case, which was still almost daily.

Within a week we were able to pull together enough money to cover all the costs of Matthew's service. We couldn't have done it without the help of our family, friends and even complete strangers.

Matthew's service was scheduled to be at Our Lady of Fatima, the same Portuguese church that our family had used for every celebratory and memorial service for as long as I could remember.

Chapter Seven
FUNERAL—EXPENSES AND EMOTION

It is light grief that can take counsel.

~ Anonymous ~

I was a wreck the days leading up to Matthew's funeral service. I was not sleeping or eating, and I was falling apart emotionally and physically. I couldn't concentrate on anything for long periods of time, as my mind constantly wandered. I couldn't focus enough to read anything, and I definitely couldn't watch television, as everything reminded me of Matthew. I paced constantly throughout the day and night, so much so that my calves ached all the time.

Mitchell's thirteenth birthday came and went just eight days after Matthew was murdered, and not one of us remembered. It would be my sisters who realized it, so they decided to have a little family birthday party for him at my sister Tina's house, to cheer him up. Even with all their efforts at trying to provide him with some normalcy, none of us could bring ourselves to sing "Happy Birthday" when his cake was brought out. I will never forget how sad Mitchell and Braydan looked as they stood together, looking at the candles on the cake. When Mitchell was asked to make a wish and blow out his candles, we all knew what that wish was, but it was one wish none of us could make come true.

A few days before the service, I got a frantic call from the priest at the parish who wanted me to know that the media had somehow found out that Matthew's service was going to be there, and they were asking him for more details. I thought, by the sound of panic in his voice, that he was about to ask us to have the service elsewhere but I was relieved to hear that all he wanted was instructions on how to deal with the media. I pleaded with him not to give out any information as to when or what time the service was going to be held, as this was the one time I did not want the media around. I wanted Matthew's service to be as private as possible, and I wanted to be able to mourn him without the cameras rolling.

The morning of the service, we all began to prepare ourselves to leave for the church. This was done in complete silence. The boys dressed themselves in their black suits while I tried to find enough strength to pull on my own clothing. It was all just too unbelievable to explain, like we were all walking zombies just going through the motions, trying to make it to the end of the day. We drove to my aunt's house in Burnaby to meet with my family, and to save the cost on the limousines having to pick us up all over the lower mainland. We all got into the cars and made our way to the church for Matthew's service. I stared out the window into the dark clouds looming overhead. This day, like the day of Matthew's death, was raining and grey, although most of July had been scorching and bright. I remember vividly how hard it rained the morning we left the hospital. I wondered if it was a sign. I wondered if the heavens were also mourning along with us.

We drove past so many places that reminded me of Matthew. The Shoppers Drug Mart where he had worked as a cashier, his high school, his favourite places to hang out with his friends. I could not keep myself from wondering, *What would he be doing right now?* I was in absolute denial, even though I was in the car on the way to his service. I could not wrap my brain around the fact that Matthew was gone, and that he would never be at his usual places again. Trying to apply logic to any of the thoughts I was having was purely irrational, since nothing in my life made any sense at this point. Trying to tell myself that I needed to accept what had happened was even crazier, as I could not even bring myself to acknowledge that Matthew was dead—let alone murdered. Things like this were not supposed to happen to my family, let alone my children. We are good people, the kind of people who help others. Law-abiding, educated, hard-working people—this wasn't supposed to happen to us, was it?

We arrived outside the church and were asked by the funeral director to remain in the car until all those paying their respects had been seated. I was struck by the hundreds of friends and family who had come to say their final goodbyes. The church quickly filled to its capacity, leaving those arriving late to stand against the walls, throughout the foyer and outside the main doors. The front doors were left open so that those who could not make their way inside the church could hear the service for Matthew.

The car door was slowly opened and I looked up to see the funeral director reaching out for my hand, telling me it was time to begin the service. I sat quietly for a moment wondering how I was going to get through it, and afraid to see Matthew's casket being pulled out from the rear of the hearse parked in front of the church. He took my hand in his and I allowed him to guide me to where I needed to be for the procession that was about to begin.

The moment the rear door was opened and Matthew's casket was in sight, I was hit again by the weight of my loss. It seemed surreal to me to think that my beautiful little boy lay inside the shiny oblong box. I had thoughts of trying to pry it open to see him once again, but Mitchell and Braydan held my hands firmly in theirs, tears streaming down their little faces.

The pallbearers on each side of Matthew's casket were David, my brothers-in-law Alan and Boris, my cousins Dave and Jose, and my nephew, Danny. I will never forget that each of them had the same stoic frozen expression on their faces.

Ave Maria began to play and everyone rose as the priest blessed the casket at the entrance of the parish. I stood at the very end of the casket as the ritual was being performed, feeling tiny splashes of holy water bounce off the casket onto the tops of our hands. I was handed a crucifix by the funeral director, who motioned to hand it to the priest to have blessed. Once it was blessed, it was returned to me as a remembrance to take home and hang for Matthew. This crucifix now hangs above his baby sister's crib, a constant reminder of the life that Matthew never had the chance to enjoy.

The service was attended by hundreds. Matthew's friends from school, some as far back as elementary school, lined the walls. Homicide investigators, coworkers, colleagues, and family we had not seen in years, had made the effort. There were some my husband had never even met—all were there to pay their respects.

The service was performed first in English, and then in Portuguese, for our family and friends who could not understand or follow along. Matthew was remembered for his kind heart, and his ability to love people from all walks of life. Looking around the church at all the different and unique friends he had, made you completely understand.

David was asked to deliver Matthew's eulogy, and throughout his reading the wailing could be heard from every corner of the church. I wasn't able to take my eyes off of Matthew's casket, which sat just a few feet from me, at the front of the church. I kept asking myself if it was really my son in there. I wondered if all the things I had given to the funeral director to place in his little drawer were really there. I was in absolute disbelief and denial, and nothing seemed to dull the ache in my heart.

After the eulogy, David returned to his seat beside me, and I quickly hid my face in his chest and cried uncontrollably. What was I doing here? I wanted to go back in time to try and change the events of that tragic day. Why hadn't I told Matthew he was forbidden to watch the fireworks? Why wasn't I there to hug him and kiss him before he left? All of these thoughts raced through my head all at once, and nothing I did could shake the guilt that consumed me.

The wave of emotions built as the service came to a close, perhaps because I knew that the next stop would be the final one; the cemetery. As we left our seats and were ushered towards the doors, there seemed a crush of people reaching out to try and comfort us, a wall of well-meaning hands and tear-streaked faces. The distance from our pew to the entrance of the church seemed a marathon, stretching out along an endless corridor. My husband and I became two separate centers of an ever-growing crowd, as people pressed in and swirled around us to offer their respects, shake hands, and hug. Voices were hushed and subdued, but I recall the ever-present sound of weeping, as my sisters and I were inconsolable, wailing in anguish.

We eventually made it back to the limos and were seated. We waited while the hearse came around from the rear of the church and the funeral procession made its solemn way towards the graveyard. Nobody spoke much during the drive, with the only noise the sound of raindrops falling from the heavens.

By the time we reached the cemetery, there were already hundreds gathered by Matthew's final resting place. I remained in the car and watched as the pallbearers carried my son's casket, placing it upon straps that would soon lower him into the ground. Once they had done so, I slowly forced myself out of the car; I had to will my body to move in closer. I was terrified by what I was watching, and slowly my brain began to fill with a thick fog, causing everything and everyone around me to disappear.

The only thing I can vaguely remember is watching people come up one-by-one to drop earth onto Matthew's casket. A young man, who I assumed to be a friend of Matthew's, stood before Matthew's casket, took off his own necklace and spoke to Matthew. He tossed his necklace into the grave. I almost fell to the ground watching him; I could no longer take it. It was at this point that I completely shut down, because I stood and walked to the car, leaving everyone behind. They had begun to slowly lower Matthew's casket into the ground. I was not going to watch it happen. I knew that, had I stayed to watch, I would have flung myself into the ground with him.

I would write letters to Matthew almost daily, leaving a few of them on a memorial tribute website made for our family and Matthew's friends. I want to share the first letter I left him just sixteen days after his murder, and three days after his funeral service.

Letter to Matthew

July 18, 2005

My Beautiful Son,

It has been 16 days since you left us, and my heart aches to hold you, and hear your beautiful voice. I can do nothing more but count the days since we last touched. I would give anything just to hold you and tell you how proud I am to be your mom.

You have taught me so much; tolerance and acceptance of those who are different, and to never judge those we do not know. You are truly a gift to all of us, and all those you knew. I cry for you every day, I call out for you and I feel you here with me, telling me everything will be okay.
I hope I never failed you as a mother, I hope I was everything you ever wanted and needed. I wish it had been me boo, but God chose you this time baby, to be by his side, to share your songs of love.

Your little brothers miss you so, and your dogs miss you too. Tigger still sleeps on your bed and keeps your pillow warm for you. I love you baby boy now and forever. Mommy will fight for you for the rest of my life, I will make sure this will never ever happen again Matty. If we can save one child in your memory, I will do it boo…I promise you…

I love you, baby boy!!

Mom, Dad and your Brothers

p.s. Please watch over the baby in my tummy, keep her safe now and always…

Chapter Eight

AND LIFE GOES ON—
IF THAT'S WHAT YOU CALL IT

The heart is forever inexperienced.

~ Henry David Thoreau ~

*T*he days and months after Matthew passed away are a bit of a blur for me. The only way I can describe how I managed to cope, was that I became a completely different person. A stranger began to live in my body, carrying out my daily routine, going through the motions of life, completely oblivious to the isolation I was creating.

I spent many days in bed contemplating my life, watching the minutes and hours passing by, only to be stricken by the most intense physical pain for the child I was carrying. I needed something to keep me going, anything to take my mind off the grief, so that I could take care of this baby suffering inside me. I was so angry with God. How could he have taken Matthew, while I was pregnant with a sibling he would never know? I began to feel as though it was his idea of a big joke. God would take Matthew from me, and then try and make me feel better by giving me another baby. As crazy as it may sound, this is exactly what I was thinking. It felt like a terribly cruel joke that I wanted nothing to do with. I wanted them both, not just one or the other.

My monthly visit to our family doctor was a wake-up call for me. I was not gaining enough weight, and the baby was smaller than it should have been, in relation to how far along I was. What was I doing? Why was I allowing this baby to suffer due to something that was beyond its control? David was terrified that we would lose our baby, and he knew that if I miscarried, it would be enough to send me off the deep end.

From that moment on, I began to be more conscious of my food consumption. Within a few weeks, I was able to catch up on all the weight necessary to be considered a normal pregnancy weight. I also decided to keep myself busy by beginning to paint the nursery, and buying the baby's furniture for the room. I begged our family doctor to let me know the sex of our baby, so I could begin to focus on something other than the grief. I had an ultrasound already booked for later that week, and thought I would take advantage of it by finding out if we were going to have a boy or a girl. My doctor agreed, but let us know that mistakes have been made before, so we were not to rely solely on the ultrasound for answers. This was an exception to what has become the rule, at least here in British Columbia. Doctors rarely tell parents the sex of the baby until well into the third trimester, to prevent people from aborting the pregnancy if the child is not the desired sex.

While I waited the duration of the week for my ultrasound appointment, I was struck by how upset I became whenever I thought about how I would feel if I had another boy. I didn't want another boy, as I felt that this was a spiteful plan to replace Matthew. I realize how thick this must sound, but it was in fact what I was thinking.

David and I arrived at the ultrasound clinic feeling anxious and excited. It is amazing how one can feel such sadness and happiness at the same time. I had never experienced anything quite like it, so from one moment to the next I was an emotional wreck.

Once my name had been called, we were ushered into a dark little room, the technician handed me a gown and a blanket and ask that I lie supine on the bed. He left the room to allow me the privacy to undress and get settled. Once I was ready I pulled out a picture of Matthew that I always carried with me, lying down, clutching it over my heart. I wanted Matthew to be with me for this, if only in spirit. Moments later the technician returned to begin the ultrasound.

The tears streamed down my face as the ultrasound began. Seeing this baby for the first time stirring within me—even in two dimensions on the screen—was overwhelming. The technician pointed out the heart, and you could see the little chambers pumping life into its body. It was all so very surreal, my fingers tightened over Matthew's picture, and I sobbed even harder. The technician was shocked, unsure if he had done or said something wrong.

I unfurled my fingers from the photo and showed the technician Matthew's picture, telling him I had recently lost my son in a random and violent murder. I also told him that it was my wish to know the sex of the baby in my womb, so I could try to divert my attention from the grief. He immediately began to scan the screen and took some pictures, telling us he would do all he could to find the sex of the baby for us.

He left the room and told us he would be back with the results. Within minutes, he returned with a few ultrasound photos for us, and told us we were going to have a baby girl. David and I looked at one another, and, as if in unison, we exhaled months' worth of stress and worry.

Now that we knew we were having a little girl, we began to plan in earnest for her arrival. The name chosen for our daughter was Chhaya Isabella, in part because this was one from a list of possibilities we had drawn up months before, when Matthew was still alive, and the one he liked. We later learned the meaning of the name; Chhaya comes from an ancient Hindi scripture and means "shadow" or "a copy of an image from above."

Our baby girl arrived on January 16, 2006, and brought a much-needed light into our lives. Caring for a newborn kept us busy and focused on her needs, and those first few months of her life sped by. Accompanying the joy we felt, was, of course, the continued sense of loss. We could not reconcile these mixed feelings sometimes, and I often felt a quiet anguish or guilt at the pleasures of watching the baby grow.

The one-year anniversary of Matthew's death was upon us, and we held a special tribute for him at the cemetery, along with many friends and family. We spoke of our remembrance of him, and released balloons into the sky, each with his name or a personal message written on them.

It would only be a few days after we marked this first year anniversary that any sense of serenity would be ripped from me forever.

Chapter Nine
THE ACCUSED SEEK BAIL

There will be no justice
as long as man will stand with a knife or with a gun
and destroy those who are weaker than he is.

~ Isaac Bashevis Singer ~

*O*n July 4th, 2006, Katherine Quinn, one of the accused in my young son's murder, would be granted bail and released on a $5,000 surety. This would be the day that my family felt the earth being ripped out from under our feet. I could not believe that they would release someone accused of murdering a child on a mere $5,000. By comparison, we have seen white collar criminals who embezzle money from clients having to come up with over $100,000 for bail. Wasn't my child's life worth more than that? The sad fact is that this bail condition is imposed on the accused, and is established by the courts to reflect their financial circumstances.

What a disgrace!

Shouldn't the fee be high enough so that they can't get out, so they have to struggle to be able to obtain the money? Lord knows our family was struggling financially to keep ourselves afloat. Even a year after Matthew's death, my husband and I were still paying off the loans we incurred in order to bury our child and pay our bills. We had lost my income as I still was not capable of working, due to the stress I was feeling.

I did try to go back to work on a few occasions, even though I was far from ready to return, emotionally or mentally. The doctors I had worked for before working at the hospital offered me my position back at the clinic, but I just couldn't do it anymore. I couldn't seem to focus on what I was doing. I was still grieving the loss. I was still wandering in a dark place and far too raw to care for myself, let alone someone else.

My husband was forced back to work just eight weeks after Matthew's death; we were on the verge of losing everything we had worked so hard for. David and I just could not seem to catch our breath after everything we had been through. The bills just kept coming, and there was nothing we could do to stop them.

My son's funeral cost just under thirty thousand dollars; a very simple and basic funeral. The four thousand dollars the government had given us to help absorb some of the funeral costs was a slap in the face. The maximum amount given to a family to help pay for a funeral in B.C. is five thousand dollars.

(Funeral assistance is something F.A.C.T., well into its second year, has begun to address.)

Katherine Quinn had already spent a year in prison awaiting the trial for my son's murder when we were notified, less than twenty-four hours before, of the bail hearing. For those of you who have never had to deal with the National Parole Board of Canada, or any other agency that is supposed to notify you of these things, last-minute notification is common practice. I have even received letters in the mail after the fact, after Matthew's killers have already been escorted outside the prison, for Lord-knows-what reasons.

We are not entitled as victims/families to know anything about the accused, let alone the convicted. Our Canadian Charter of Rights is only there to protect the criminals, not the law-abiding citizens of Canada. Criminals enjoy all the rights and privileges entrenched within the constitution, but suffer little consequence for their actions.

I was still reeling from the loss of my son, and the birth of his little sister. I was just two months pregnant when Matthew was killed. I was consumed by guilt throughout the pregnancy. The stress and shock were taking a toll on me, and it was a miracle the baby survived the trauma of it all. I cannot even to begin to tell you how hard it was for me to deal with. I had lost a child, and brought another child into this world all at the same time.

I was not prepared to allow the justice system to fail my little boy and our family—it was all just too much to bear.

The judge who released Quinn on bail didn't even take into consideration the fact that he was releasing her into the custody of her parents, who lived ten blocks from our family's home.

The Last Six Minutes

We were shocked by the outcome. Never did we believe that this could happen. Never did we believe that one of our son's killers would be living minutes from our front door.

The very next day, I contacted my Victims' Services worker to ask her about having a security alarm/panic button installed in our home, as it was one of the things listed on their webpage as a service provided for victims/families. She told me that she would look into it and get back to me as soon as she knew if it was possible. I couldn't see why I wouldn't be able to have a security alarm, as I feared for my safety and the safety of my children. With David back to work at his corporate security job and travelling like crazy trying to catch up on all the time he had already missed from work, it meant that I was quite often left alone.

I heard back from my worker the very next day. I wasn't prepared for what she was about to tell me. I was told that I did not qualify for the security system. I was never really given a reason as to why they'd refused me, and I remember asking her what I had to do to qualify for the system. Did I need to lose another child before I would be protected? None of it made any sense. I almost felt as though the government agencies were less than useless.

The bail conditions did nothing to pacify us. It was an absolute joke! I can't tell you how many times I drove past the Quinn's street while she was in her parents' custody, praying that I would catch her breaching her conditions. I honestly don't know what I would have done had I come face-to-face with her. Would I have run her over with my car? Perhaps, but truthfully, I don't believe I could have ever followed through with it—I just like to think I could have.

That was when it hit me—I had to do something. What it was—I had no idea, but I could no longer stand by and watch my life spiral out of control. I vividly remember sitting in the tub—screaming at the top of my lungs, crying uncontrollably, not able to comprehend what was happening. I felt as though my days consisted of nothing more than tears and sadness. My husband could do nothing to console me.

I was on the verge of a nervous breakdown, and there was nothing anyone could say or do to help me. All I could do was look at my surviving children and pray that I would not lose my mind. I needed to search deep within myself for some strength—anything that could keep me from slipping into a terrible depression. If I allowed that to happen, I knew it would be the end. I couldn't do that to David or my children. They had suffered enough already; they didn't need to lose another member of our family.

I began to think of what I could do to get people's attention about what had just happened. I had heard of people holding rallies outside the courthouses for these types of judicial blunders before. I knew we could get enough people together for support and help, but I had no idea if it could actually work. Matthew's murder had been a very high-profile case, and every local media outlet had followed his story quite closely. They had asked us to keep them posted on anything that was happening in regards to the murderers and the pending trial. Due to this, my husband and I had made some friends in the media, so we took a chance and called as many of them as we could to tell them what we were about to do, and about Quinn's release. Even if we could do nothing about her release, at least we could let others know how the system had failed Matthew and his family.

Chapter Ten

THE PROTESTS BEGIN—
CRIMINAL JUSTICE ON TRIAL

The dead cannot cry out for justice;
it is a duty of the living to do so for them.

~ Lois McMaster Bujold ~

*J*ust days after Quinn's release, about fifty people rallied alongside my family in front of the New Westminster Courthouse. The media came out as well to hear our family's cries over the release, and to ask our government to impose stricter bail laws. The sheriffs at the courthouse were expecting us, having heard the announcement of the rally mentioned on the radio. They came out to greet us, and after speaking with my family, realized we were there for a peaceful protest, and not to cause them any problems. They were encouraging of our cause.

We all carried signs or wore placards around our necks voicing our concerns. Everything from "Justice for Matthew" to "No Bail for Matthew's Killers." It was at this very rally that I would meet Nina Rivet, a woman who had lost not one, but two of her loved ones to violent acts of crime. Nina had heard about the rally through a friend who had heard about it on the news. She had also lost her son just months after Matthew was murdered.

Nina had already spent many years within the court system trying to fight for the deportation of the two street racers convicted of the death of her sister, Irene Thorpe. Nina knew first-hand how one becomes disillusioned by the courts and the government agencies. She had seen how victims were left to fend for themselves in the chaos.

Nina had worked alongside the Member of Parliament, Chuck Cadman, on amendments to the Criminal Code to create harsher penalties for street racing. Cadman was a strong advocate for crime victims—he was one himself. We had hoped to contact Mr. Cadman to see if he could help us. In a strange twist of fate, Chuck died of cancer just days after Matthew was killed. He had also created a group for victims and their families in 1993, called Crime, Responsibility & Youth, (C.R.Y.) C.R.Y. was created after his own sixteen-year-old son Jesse was murdered in a situation similar to our son's.

With common ground and common goals, it seemed natural for Nina and me to begin discussing plans for a new organization, one that would address the needs of victims of crime. Within weeks we had met with close friends and family around our dining room table.

We discussed every aspect of how F.A.C.T. would run, and how we would help others like ourselves. In August of 2006, Families Against Crime & Trauma, (F.A.C.T.) was born.

Rumina Daya, a reporter and one of our close contacts from Global News, called us and offered to feature F.A.C.T. on their Labour Day weekend broadcast. This would be a fairly lengthy piece that served as a great launch for our fledgling organization. Within seconds of the segment ending, our phone began to ring. My husband and I were both sitting in front of the television with our children, and at that moment we just looked at one another in awe. I remember being too nervous to answer the call, so David took it. It was a woman who had survived a terrible assault, and she wanted to know how she could join the organization. I couldn't believe it—we had our very first member.

Global News had also featured our email address during the piece, and by the next morning, Nina and I had received hundreds of letters from across Canada. These were families who had lost loved ones to violent acts: they also felt as though they were alone in their grief, and in their fight to win justice. We even received letters from those who had never been personally touched; these people just wanted to offer support to our cause. It took us days to get through all the letters we had received, but we answered each and every one of them.

I'd also begun to search for a man named Wallace Gilby Craig. One of the doctors I'd worked with had heard him speak on a local radio show about the broken criminal justice system. He was promoting his new book, called, "Short Pants to Striped Trousers." Mr. Craig wrote about his years as a provincial court judge, the lack of government leadership and the failings of the criminal justice system.

I found his webpage with his contact information, and I wrote him a very detailed letter about our loss, and everything that we were doing with F.A.C.T. I asked him for advice, and hoped he would be willing to help us in our fight to see changes made not only to the way victims and their families were being treated, but also to the criminal justice system. Mr. Craig responded to my letter, and from that moment on, we have kept in close touch with one another. Mr. Craig came to my home just weeks later to sit with the members of F.A.C.T. during a meeting. I was immediately taken with his impressive knowledge, his compassion and his kindness.

Mr. Craig brought with him copies of his book for everyone at our meeting, and spoke at great length with us about what he felt needed to be done, and how we could achieve these goals. Within months, he would become my friend and mentor, a man who would teach me more than I could have ever possibly imagined. Mr. Craig contacted me after our first meeting and asked my permission to write about us in his next column in the North Shore News, where he had a monthly column that discussed law and order, and current issues.

The article was published on July 4th, 2007, one year after Quinn's release on bail. It was called "Victims Organize for Justice." Mr. Craig began the article by speaking about the aftermath of violent crime, citing R. v. Cookman, one of the criminal cases he presided over during his time as a judge. I include the last few paragraphs of his article:

...A decade later I sense that victims of crime are making their presence felt by confronting prosecutors, judges and politicians. They are beginning to stand together as activists in a fight to have true enforcement of the Criminal Code in terms of the sentencing of violent offenders.

A most amazing coming together of victims was triggered by the July 2, 2005 murder of diminutive 16-year-old Matthew Martins. Young Martins was beaten to death by Robert Forslund, a frenzied psychopathic criminal, urged on by his co-accused girlfriend Katherine Quinn.

It was barbarism so fierce it would make a terrorist quake. It was a murder that justified a death penalty.

Somehow, grief-stricken Sandra Martins-Toner and David Toner galvanized themselves to perpetuate the memory of their son Matthew through a public crusade for justice; first, in the case against Forslund and Quinn, and beyond that in coalescing with other victims in "an organization of families who have lost loved ones tragically, or for those who have survived a violent crime."

They are F.A.C.T.: Families Against Crime & Trauma, a group to be reckoned with, a grass roots organization that is in the ascendancy and has caught the attention of judges and politicians.

61

F.A.C.T. members are truly one for all and all for one. They will not settle for a "purple heart." Their goal is an end to lax sentences and the revolving-door court system. They want hard-nosed prosecutors and law-and-order judges.

I will never forget my first meeting with them in the Martins-Toner home. It seemed like a gathering of a clan. As our discussion progressed, I realized that I was the only one in the room who had not suffered the murder of a loved one.

I left in awe and with a feeling of optimism that victims of crime will succeed in restoring balance to the scales of justice.

Yet I will always feel deeply for them over their circumstances: that in the quiet of solitude and dreamy reverie there will be moments of whispering melancholy and tears.

—Wallace G. Craig

This prompted Nina and me to reach out to others, not only in our province, but across Canada. We asked each and every one of them if they had felt re-victimized by the criminal justice system, and the government victim's services programs. I wanted to know if I was the only one who had felt this way, or had been treated this unfairly. I had no idea that through our work with F.A.C.T., we were about to expose these government agencies for their ineffectuality in providing financial help and resources for victims/families.

Chapter Eleven

SKYTRAIN IMPROVEMENTS—
ACTIVISM REWARDED

*You desire to know the art of living, my friend? It is contained
in one phrase: make use of suffering.*

~ Henri-Frédéric Amiel ~

Shortly after Matthew's murder, David and I realized that, had
there been some type of security at the SkyTrain Station, perhaps
Matthew's life could have been saved. I sometimes wonder if that
was why he had run towards the station in the first place. We
would find out that there were many witnesses to his murder, but
unfortunately, other than two young girls, not a single one of them
did anything to protect or rescue Matthew. These young girls had
their lives threatened by Forslund for trying to stop him. He had
taken the girls' identification from them and told them that if they
ever spoke to anyone about what they had observed, he would find
them and kill them.

I'm sure you are asking yourself how he could have gotten their ID, but you have to remember what these girls had just witnessed, and how afraid they were when he told them to hand over their information.

The two girls were not able to save my son that night, but I will never forget the bravery and courage they showed. I can't even imagine the guilt they must live with, having seen my son murdered. My family has had the chance to meet them on a few occasions, and I will never forget the look in their eyes. I think of them often, and pray that Matthew will watch over them and keep them safe. They must carry a terrible burden that will hang heavy over their hearts for the rest of their lives.

Another young man, in his early thirties, who had witnessed the entire beating couldn't get himself to intervene out of sheer terror and shock. He would be the one to identify Quinn and Forslund to the police later that morning.

Had it not been for this same man, Forslund and Quinn might have gotten away with the murder, or at least until the police had linked them to the people on the surveillance tape. This in itself could have been a lengthy investigation, and it could have taken months—if not years—to capture them. He left the scene of the crime as he heard the paramedics and sirens approaching, but before leaving, he walked toward Matthew's crumpled body and told Matthew to hold on: help was on its way. The reason he left was that there was an outstanding warrant for his arrest, and he was afraid of being taken into custody.

He then turned and retreated into the mall parking lot, all the time wondering what he could do to help Matthew. He assumed that the paramedics would take Matthew to the nearest hospital, so he began to walk the twenty minutes required to the emergency ward of Surrey Memorial Hospital. Once he arrived at the entrance, he noticed seven police cruisers. One of the cruisers had a man in the back seat. The witness knew immediately that it was the same man he had seen beating Matthew. He approached a female officer standing outside the doors, and asked her if the scene had anything to do with what had happened at the Surrey Central SkyTrain Station. She told him to stay put, and then proceeded to get her supervisor. When the female officer returned with her supervisor, the man then told him that the person in the back of the cruiser, Forslund, was the one responsible for the assault at the station. He then noticed Quinn leaving the emergency ward, escorted by an officer. That was when he also identified her as one of Matthew's assailants.

The rest of the witnesses were either drug addicts hanging around the station, or those who wouldn't get involved. We later found out that there was a Translink employee, a janitor, who could be seen in the surveillance video while the assault was taking place, cleaning. Unbelievably, the man pretended not to notice what was happening, and continued with his duties.

I can't imagine seeing something like that happening and not doing something to try to intervene. These are just a few of the thoughts that I'm plagued with on a daily basis. I am haunted by so many unanswered questions from that tragic night.

We also found out that we were very lucky the police officers had been quick to grab the surveillance tape, as the system Translink was using was outdated. It looped back the video caught by the cameras every few hours. This was unacceptable to us. We couldn't believe that a billion dollar corporation was using such an antiquated CCTV system. Had it not been for the quick thinking of the officers, our child's murderers would probably have never seen any jail time. This situation really opened our eyes to the lack of safety and security in place at these high crime, public, locations.

David and I began to pressure Translink through letter writing and the media to update the system they had been using. It wasn't an easy battle: we couldn't have done it without the support of the public, and the NDP MLA, Adrian Dix.

The level of violence in or around the stations was increasing significantly. Translink tried to slough it off by saying that the crimes were happening close to the stations, and not on their property, but that did nothing to comfort the riders, who feared for their safety. We discovered that some stations experienced higher levels of crime, so those were the ones we targeted first, including Surrey Central Station where Matthew was killed.

MLA Adrian Dix created a ten-point plan that we would support in order to pressure the government and Translink to make changes to the stations. We participated in a petition-signing campaign at several SkyTrain stations, covered extensively by the media, keeping the pressure on the Transit Authority.

Sandra Martins-Toner

On August 1st, 2008, the long-promised and debated upgrades to SkyTrain security were completed. They included things such as improved lighting and new digital video surveillance systems that would allow captured images to be accessed for seven consecutive days. We felt elated, as if we had slain a giant. The mighty Translink had been successfully lobbied by social pressure. This success confirmed that we were on the right track.

Chapter Twelve
GUARDIAN ANGELS—
COMMITMENT TO COMMUNITY

*I wanted you to see what real courage is, instead
of getting the idea that courage is a man with a gun in his hand.
It's when you know you're licked before you begin
but you begin anyway and you see it through
no matter what.*

~ Harper Lee, *To Kill a Mockingbird* ~

While we worked on these initiatives, David began looking into other methods of safety and security for the public. After hearing a radio piece about the famous Guardian Angels safety patrol coming to Vancouver to establish a chapter, he sent an email to the leader of the Toronto chapter. David explained the circumstances of our loss, and offered his assistance. The founder of the Angels, Curtis Sliwa, was interested. Curtis was very receptive to the idea of resurrecting the group again in Vancouver and other parts of the lower mainland. Before long, David was in touch with former members of the Vancouver group. We were not too sure how the communities would feel about having these "red-beret-clad vigilantes" roaming the streets of Vancouver again. The Guardian Angels received a very cold reception from the police when they originally started up, in the late eighties. I use the term vigilantes, but the Angels are nothing more than the eyes and ears for our police officers, like any other community safety group. I think they had gotten a really bad rap in the mid-eighties due to a few members who took things a little too far in the U.S., but really, the group was composed mainly of average people trying to keep order in their neighbourhoods.

Curtis Sliwa flew in from New York at the end of July, 2006, to meet with David and police officials at a press conference in Vancouver. David was very eager to re-establish a chapter in the city, but he also knew it would be hard work trying to convince others.

The Guardian Angels, who describe themselves as a community safety group, had operated on the streets of Vancouver from 1987 to 1992. During the latter part of the 1990's, the group lost momentum, as many of the members married and moved on to professional careers.

Back in the present, David volunteered to take on the position of chapter leader and the group began recruiting members and training them. My husband seemed the ideal person for this. He not only had a personal interest in fighting crime due to our horrible loss, but fulfilled the professional qualifications as a security expert and martial arts instructor. He knew what he was doing.

Recruiting people to become citizen patrollers proved more difficult than it should have been. Many people voiced support; few turned out for patrol. Could it be that Vancouverites were just too apathetic about crime in their city to care? Many said they had problems in their neighbourhoods, but wanted nothing to do with actually getting out there and cleaning up their own streets. Some condo complexes and strata organizations even offered the Angels money to patrol their properties, something they could have just hired a private security company for. The Angels, of course, refused.

"That isn't how it's done," said David. "People have to take an active responsibility for their own communities."

Despite establishing positive relations with the Vancouver Police and SkyTrain Security, the group struggled to train and field enough members to create a solid presence in the community. All the while, Families Against Crime & Trauma grew stronger and spread like wildfire across the country. David was doing double duty, also serving as the public affairs coordinator for F.A.C.T. and doing constant media spots and interviews. He was having to change hats between the Angels, F.A.C.T. and his everyday job.

David's profession, ironically enough, was ensuring the safety and security of a large retail corporation. As a retail loss prevention specialist and investigator, he often thought it a bizarre twist of fate that someone with his background would lose a child to a criminal act. And now, he was viewing the justice system from the perspective of a victim.

Within a few months, the competing interests of the Angels, F.A.C.T. and work began to stretch him too thin; he had to make a choice.

One other underlying issue exacerbated the situation—my own fears. I had become so anxious that, every time David left the house to run a patrol, I would call him every fifteen minutes, and beg him to come home. I couldn't stand the thought of something happening to him while out patrolling the streets. How could this be? Here I was screaming for people to do something—anything—to reduce the level of crime, but I did not want my husband involved. Not personally, at the street level.

In February of 2007, with the trial for the accused in Matthew's murder looming only one month away, David regretfully stepped down as the chapter leader and left the Guardian Angels. It was a difficult decision for him, but he stated, "I've accomplished my goal—the chapter is established and patrols are running regularly. I can now focus on the larger goal of changing laws and working with our politicians."

We knew that the weeks ahead would take a heavy emotional toll on our family, and we began to focus ourselves on the trial.

Chapter Thirteen
THE TRIAL BEGINS

The one who throws the stone forgets;
the one who is hit remembers forever.

~ *Angolan Proverb* ~

*M*arch 14, 2007, marked the first day of trial for Matthew's killers. Coincidentally, a few weeks before our own trial beginning, the trial for Robert "Willy" Pickton began in the same courthouse. The man known as Canada's most prolific serial killer, a pig farmer from Port Coquitlam, B.C., was being tried one floor below ours for the murder of six women, the first of twenty-six sex trade workers he was accused of killing.

Between the Pickton trial and the trial for Matthew's killers, the stage was set for a media frenzy. Tents were erected outside the main doors, and a podium awaited us for a press conference as soon as we arrived. For the first few days of the trial, we couldn't step out the doors without facing the media. With dozens of microphones and audio recorders thrust in our faces, we tried our best to remain calm.

It would still be at least a week before the jury would be brought in. Our little girl was just fourteen months old, a beacon of light in all our darkness. I had been consumed by terror in the weeks leading up to this day, and lack of sleep was not helping my anxieties. At a time when a family should be rejoicing in the new life they had created, we could do nothing but fear the unknown. I felt as though my life no longer belonged to me. So much of the past year and a half was just a blur to me—precious moments lost in an abyss of anguish. It was as if I were standing outside my body, watching everything happening, and there was nothing I could do to regain control.

We learned a few weeks before the trial that the accused had chosen a trial by judge and jury. We didn't know what to think of the decision, as we had heard that many times it's a strategy to gain sympathy from the jurors.

I wanted to think that anyone who could sit through the gruesome details of a child's death couldn't be sympathetic to the murderers, but I also understood that the defence counsel would try to have the jury interpret the events of that night as if Matthew had done something to deserve the beating.

My family attended the first day of court without me. We had been told that the jury wouldn't be present on the first day; that it would only be the Crown prosecutors and defence lawyers entering the submissions obtained during the *voir dire*, and any decisions that had been made during the preliminary hearings, weeks before the trial.

Nina Rivet sat alongside my family every single day during the trial. She took notes on everything that she heard or saw, in order to keep a record for our family and our organization.

These notes even went so far as to include the facial expressions, movements and even occasional flatulence of the accused. Why she felt the need to report on these details I will never know, but I can tell you that it broke up the monotony of sitting in a cold, hard courtroom. Nina doesn't miss a thing, and nothing will ever escape her watchful eye.

A former restaurant owner, Nina was injured several years ago in a car accident, which left her on permanent disability and resulted in the loss of her business. After the death of her sister, she began to educate herself about the justice system, always taking a common sense approach and an "I can do it" attitude. For someone without the benefit of a college education, she has nonetheless made quite a reputation for herself in the local courthouses, and has on more than one occasion made a hot-shot lawyer look foolish in front of his peers.

She has been able to guide many families through the convoluted court system; she does this on her own time, and without financial compensation.

Most families have learned through this process that trying to obtain the legal transcripts of the trials can not only be a bureaucratic nightmare, but unbelievably expensive. I know that in my own case, there are at least over twelve volumes, and the cost could vary from eight hundred dollars, up to three thousand dollars. Nina now takes notes for every family whose trials we attend. We hand the notes over at the end of the trial, or when the family is ready to read through the documents.

It was very important for us throughout the trial process to try to hold each other's spirits up. The time we had already spent in the courthouse had granted us wonderful relationships with those who worked there.

The sheriffs had also followed our family's story, and gave us the support and strength to continue pursuing justice for Matthew. Although they could never voice their personal thoughts on what had happened to our son, you could see the sorrow in their eyes.

A friend of the family had hundreds of buttons made with Matthew's picture on them, and the words "Justice for Matthew." Everyone who attended the trial wore one, and others in the community wore them in support of Matthew and the family.

In the week that followed, Wendy Dawson, the Crown prosecutor, would give the jury a simple walk-through of how she would be presenting her case. Wendy seemed to glide across the courtroom floor with grace and poise, always in control of her thoughts. I think that someone up above finally decided to cut my family a break and sent her to us. With everything we had already endured—emotionally, financially and physically, we couldn't have asked for a better prosecutor. From the moment she met us, she was warm and truly caring. Had it not been for Wendy guiding us through each step, I think we would have been completely lost. I have since learned that this is not the way it always happens for families. I have heard horrific stories of prosecutors not giving families the time of day. It is sad to say, but sometimes I think they forget that our loved ones are not just names on a file they are about to prosecute. They get so caught up in the legalities that they forget to remember the pain we're in.

Wendy never seemed fazed by the defence's idiotic antics, and, let me tell you, some days we thought Quinn's lawyer, James Millar's head would explode right in front of us. Millar seemed an excitable man, and during his theatrics he would work himself into a frenzy; he'd turn five shades of red and his veins would protrude from under his skin. All we could hope for was that paramedics were positioned nearby in case he gave himself an aneurism. I have never seen so much drama in my life! I thought it only happened on TV, but boy was I wrong.

Each of the accused in our son's murder would have their own defence lawyers. Forslund's lawyer, Karen Bastow, was a little easier to endure, as she did not have that "in your face" attitude. Before the trial had ever started, Forslund's lawyer had tried to strike a deal in which he would plead guilty to second degree murder if they would allow Quinn to walk. Wendy would have none of that. There would be no deal. She felt that she had sufficient evidence to carry through the second degree murder conviction on Quinn as well.

The judge presiding in the case was Justice Selwyn Romilly, a soft-spoken Trinidadian man, well-respected by the Crown and known for his deep understanding of points of law. He spoke with a Caribbean accent, which relaxed witnesses. He occasionally joked with the jury and court staff, breaking the tension in what was a very emotionally-charged courtroom. He told several witnesses to speak up, as the appeal court was listening, alluding to the fact that his experience in murder cases made him fairly certain there would be an appeal.

Forslund's lawyer Bastow seemed to have a prior history with Justice Romilly, from a previous trial. He certainly showed very little tolerance for her attempts to defend Forslund. On many occasions, almost as soon as she left her chair to voice an objection Justice Romilly would overrule her and tell her to take her seat. This progressed almost comically over several weeks, to the point when she actually asked him one day, in an attempt at dry wit, if she should object or just remain seated.

The days that followed were filled with police officers, emergency response, doctors and witness testimonies. In total there would be twenty-seven witnesses who would take the stand. This included everyone who had had contact with Matthew before, during and after the beating. The next few weeks would only get worse, and the stress we were under was indescribable.

When I say this, you may think I am referring to what was happening inside the courtroom, but the greater and more stressful distractions were actually happening outside Room 208.

Chapter Fourteen
THE TRIAL CONTINUES

It is in justice that the ordering of society is centered.

~ Aristotle ~

*N*ot only did we have to deal with James Millar's courtroom drama, we also had to watch our son's accused killer walk around the courthouse with her family and friends in tow. I cannot even begin to describe how infuriating it was. Since she had been released on bail almost a year before the trial began, she could come and go as she pleased, in and out of the courthouse. Without knowing very much about the Quinn's, other than what we had learned through the preliminary hearings, the trial and people in the community, her family seemed the polar opposite of mine.

Quinn, a mother of three children herself, was most certainly a less-than-perfect role model for her young children. This was demonstrated by her lack of remorse from the day she killed my child, and throughout the trial. Her mother and father were present for most of the court dates until the very last few weeks, when it would just be her father. It would be on a day that her mother was present that I would come face-to-face with my son's killer.

Court had adjourned for the first break of the morning, and as I walked down the corridor with my sisters towards the stairs, I decided to use the restroom. I told my sisters that I would meet them outside. I pushed the door open—only to see Quinn and her mother standing not two feet from my face. My body began to shake; it took everything in me to physically control myself. I stared right into her cold, evil eyes and yelled, "You child killer!" Her face went stark white as I trembled just inches from her. Quinn's mother glared at me, but my eyes never left Quinn's face as her mother took her arm and ushered her out the door.

I locked myself inside the small, dark cubicle and crumpled to the floor in absolute shock and exhaustion. How could this be fair?

How could this person be allowed to walk around us, while my little boy lay in a cold grave? Once I had gathered enough strength to leave the restroom, I was met by my eldest sister Jeane and the others close behind. It seems the first thing Quinn and her mother had done after my outburst was run to Millar to tell him about the encounter. He then took it up with Crown counsel, asking her to speak to us, to keep my family in check. I think what hurt the most was my sister's reaction to what I had done.

Jeane was embarrassed at having been pulled aside and spoken to about my behaviour. I am certain that her tone with me was caused more from stress and fatigue, the weeks of being present at all the preliminary hearings, but nonetheless, I was hurt. She stated that she would not allow our family to behave in such a manner, nor would we stoop to the Quinn family's level of disrespect. She also made sure that I was aware that should I think to speak out again, our family would be removed from the courtroom for the duration of the trial.

I know that she was just being the messenger, but I think she could have gone about delivering it a little more diplomatically. Others who had heard of my outburst stated they probably would have done much worse, but regardless, I had to keep my mouth shut for the duration of the trial. To me, it just seemed unbelievably unfair.

We were made to sit just a few feet from the accused in the courtroom. Forslund would be ushered in by the sheriffs and placed into a wooden prisoner's dock with shatterproof glass halfway up, standing perhaps no higher than seven feet high. Quinn would be placed inside one of these as well, directly adjacent to Forslund's. We noted that the alleged killers had each other's names prominently tattooed on the sides of their necks in a large handwritten scrawl.

I think the thing that shocked me at seeing Forslund for the first time was his size. He was monstrous in comparison to Matthew. At the time of the assault, Forslund was six-foot-two, and weighed one-hundred-and-eighty pounds. Matthew was just five-foot-four, one-hundred-and-twenty pounds. Matthew had always been a small child, and throughout his school years he was always much smaller than his peers. The difference between him and the prime aggressor was staggering.

When Forslund stood up to be removed from the box, I was instantly struck with a physical pain in my chest. Images flashed before my eyes of him throwing my little boy around like a rag doll, and stomping on Matthew's head. I could not contain the well of emotions and instantly began to sob uncontrollably, leaning into David to hide my face. David knew exactly what had entered my thoughts, because he had also thought this same thing.

We had to sit and watch Forslund and Quinn looking at one another throughout the trial as they would try to read each other's lips, and exchange glances with one another. They made me feel nauseous. I remember sitting there, thinking that it would take nothing for me to reach over, grab Nina's pen, vault myself over the railing at the front of the benches, and plunge the pen through Forslund's jugular. I would replay the scene in my head over and over again, but of course, I would be rocked back to reality at the thought of following through with it.

That's the difference between us and them. Impulse control. We do not follow through on incredibly stupid impulses and morbid thoughts. I've never hurt anyone my entire life. I don't even think I've ever gotten a parking ticket, let alone been spoken to by authorities. We just were not raised like that. My father instilled in us girls values, morals and respect. We never disrespected or questioned our elders, we had compassion for those less fortunate, and above all, we never disobeyed the law or disrespected those in authority.

Sandra Martins-Toner

My father was a gentle man. He never felt the need to spank us, nor did we ever try and push his boundaries. I can remember many times as a young girl when my father might raise his voice, or just give me a stern look; my head would fall, and the tears would come. I could not stand the thought that I could have done something to upset my father, and I know that he felt the same way when we were upset with him.

This is why I just cannot understand Quinn's family. How could they stand by a daughter, the mother of their grandchildren, when she had brutally taken the life of another mother's child? I have to think that they somehow felt she was innocent, even after watching the video tape numerous times, and hearing witness testimony against their daughter. They steadfastly refused to accept her guilt. As the trial played on, we learned that Katherine Quinn was no stranger to the police, having been previously charged with assault and uttering threats.

At several points during the trial, Quinn, her friends and her brother actively tried to intimidate witnesses. Eventually, the brother was removed from the courtroom and told not to return.

One of the girls who tried to help Matthew the night he died was followed home and her house was vandalized. The words "Die Rat" were spray painted across her front door. Protective measures had to be taken by police for the remainder of the trial to ensure their safety. Punks.

As I work with various families through F.A.C.T., I often hear similar stories. How many criminals are never tried or convicted

83

because of witness interference or intimidation? How many families will never see the inside of a courtroom, because witnesses are too afraid to testify, or recant their stories in order to escape retaliation? This was exactly what my family began to fear.

Chapter Fifteen

THE LAST SIX MINUTES ON TAPE

There is no den in the wide world to hide a rogue. Commit a
crime and the earth is made of glass.
Commit a crime, and it seems as if a coat of snow
fell on the ground, such as reveals in the woods the track
of every partridge, and fox, and squirrel.

~ Ralph Waldo Emerson~

*C*rown counsel Wendy Dawson was always kind enough to prepare us with the key evidence that would be introduced the next day in court. One day I was advised that it would not be prudent to attend, as they would be presenting the video captured from the SkyTrain Station.

To this day I have never seen the footage, and I don't think I ever will. My family members who were present in court when it was replayed, all lowered their eyes, not wishing to see the last moments of Matthew's life played out so graphically. About the footage I can say this: it documented in approximately six minutes the repetitive attacks on my son. The black and white image, thankfully without sound, depicted an assault so savage that an experienced homicide investigator told us it made his blood boil every time he watched it. It was brought to my attention the first time the video was played for the court, that two members of the jury were weeping while they watched it. As each witness who had been present at the SkyTrain station gave their testimony, the video was played back again, as if to verify the words they spoke with an accompanying re-enactment. Only it was not a re-enactment, like some Crime Stoppersrs commercial. It was a live play-by-play of the taking of a life.

It was hard enough listening to the comments from others who had viewed it, and seeing the effect it had on them. I overheard someone say that they had not been able to shake the images from their mind. Another person said they were suffering from terrible nightmares due to the severity of the beating. I don't think they meant to say anything hurtful in my presence; it was more like they wanted to protect me from any further pain.

This very footage would become the focus of attention for the next few weeks, and it almost caused a family meltdown.

The media had inquired about the possibility of obtaining portions of the CCTV footage of Forslund assaulting Matthew to air during their news coverage of the trial. Neither David nor I were present in court that particular day, so the Crown asked my sisters and family present for their thoughts on the matter. My family was torn by the question posed; my sisters, Jeane and Sally, thought it might be a good idea to release it, while my sister, Tina, and the others present were not so keen on the idea. It was almost a done deal when Nina called me at home to advise me of what was happening. I almost fell off my chair as she told me what was about to happen. There was no way I wanted that video to become public!

With two young sons, aged ten and fourteen at home, my immediate worry was the Internet. I was afraid that footage would find its way onto YouTube and be seen by Matthew's friends and family. We all know how everything on TV ends up on the Internet, and all our kids are exposed to lots of stuff they should not see on unrestricted sites.

How could my sisters agree to releasing the video footage? I was furious that they had gone ahead without consulting me first. We had a heated debate, as they thought that publicizing the assault might help create more public awareness of the poor security standards at the SkyTrain station. It became quite clear that my sisters were not aware of the kind of information that can be obtained online. That evening after court adjourned, we phoned each other back and forth, arguing the pros and cons, while I continued to feel hurt over the whole situation.

I ultimately decided that the risk of it ending up as some sick download-of-the-week was too great. Once my family heard my reasons, they then agreed with me fully, and felt badly for ever having made a decision without informing me first. We then agreed that they wouldn't make any important decisions without my consultation and approval.

I frantically called the Crown Counsel office to protest the release, and to see if there was some way to block the media from obtaining it. Wendy Dawson understood my concerns, and suggested we come into her office in the morning to file an affidavit preventing the release. This, she cautioned us, wouldn't guarantee the media would not get access, since a Freedom of Information application might quash our affidavit, but it would make it difficult. Thankfully, we never heard any further request for the release of video, and to my knowledge, it has never been seen since the trial.

We were very grateful that the reporters and the media outlets never challenged our final decision. I couldn't imagine what I would have done if this footage had become available to the public. The thought of my children—or anyone else's children for that matter—being able to view the brutal assault that ended my child's life was unbearable.

Chapter Sixteen

KNIGHTS OF JUSTICE—
THE HOMICIDE TEAM

Justice consists not in being neutral between right and wrong,
but in finding out the right and upholding it, wherever found,
against the wrong.

~ Theodore Roosevelt ~

I cannot write this book without mentioning the homicide detectives
who worked tirelessly on our son's case. They have our deepest respect
and gratitude for the excellent police work they did. The I.H.I.T.,
which stands for Integrated Homicide Investigation Team, is a joint
task force between the RCMP and various municipal forces.

At the moment of my son's death, jurisdiction of the file
transferred from Surrey RCMP to the IHIT unit. What had been
initially reported and responded to as an assault was handed over to
the special unit once the charges were upgraded to murder.

The Last Six Minutes

The officers who work on IHIT came to our home on several occasions, to explain what was happening. They spoke to us honestly about the progress of the investigation, and called us regularly to see if we needed anything.

We noted that when they spoke about Matthew, they spoke as if they were talking about a friend, not a case or file number. I can't tell you how much this meant to David and me. They assured us that Matthew had done nothing wrong, and from what they could gather, Matthew just happened to be in the wrong place at the wrong time. They apologized for the use of this terrible cliché, but they honestly didn't know how else to put it. I have heard that cliché a hundred times since that day, and every time I do, I think of Matthew and all the other loved ones lost in random and senseless violent acts.

Members of the team interviewed Forslund and Quinn separately and segments of the interviews were given as evidence during the preliminary hearings. The interview done with Forslund the day after his arrest lasted thirteen hours, and segments of this video were played in court, which the family witnessed.

The interview began with Forslund sitting alone in an interview room for approximately ten minutes before an investigating officer from IHIT joined him. The officer placed photos of Matthew's bloodied, torn clothing in front of Forslund. Forslund immediately began to hyperventilate as he turned the photos over, so as not to see them. He then told the officer over and over again that he didn't do it—that he was not a violent person. The officer suggested that he was looking out for his girlfriend, since she had told everyone there that night that Matthew had stabbed her while she was trying to rip his chain from around his neck. It was proven in court that, not only did Matthew not stab her, but there was never any wound other than a superficial abrasion to her mid-torso. Doctors who tended to her in the emergency ward would testify that there was no stab wound. No sutures were needed, and the wound did not support her version of what had happened.

The officers would leave him alone many times throughout the process of the interrogation. Sometimes a different officer would take over the questioning. When he sat alone, Forslund would smoke his cigarettes and mumble to himself, saying that it wasn't him, that he couldn't believe that it was him, it was all in his mind. Forslund also continuously asked to be placed back into his cell, telling the officers he wanted to go home. The officers continued to assure him that it was him. They even played the video footage of him beating Matthew to death, and say to him, "this is you." He would agree that it was him in the footage, but he couldn't believe he was beating Matthew.

He continued on for hours, telling the officers he wasn't a violent person, and that he was the type who would walk away from violent situations. We should note here that in contradiction to his professed non-violent nature, police officers who arrested him outside the hospital in Surrey had to jolt him twice with a Taser in an effort to subdue him. It took four officers to restrain him, and during the scuffle, he punched one of the female officers in the face.

It was extremely emotionally exhausting for my family to sit through the interviews. We certainly could feel no pity for the monsters who took Matthew's life. Watching Forslund cry and say that he didn't do it, especially after watching the video evidence, just made everyone sick.

Quinn's interview was much briefer, and had a much different tone. It lasted approximately three hours, of which only fifty-five minutes were shown in court.

She presented much differently in the interview than Forslund. We noted that she had changed her look completely from the time of her arrest to the trial. Her hair was much darker, and you could tell that she was trying to look respectable, but to us she was still a child killer. It didn't matter what she looked like during the trial, because her true colors presented themselves quickly enough. The attitude she exhibited was evident even as the officers tried to interview her. Leaning her chair back onto its back legs and putting her feet up on the table, she was cocky, defiant and disrespectful.

At numerous times during the interview, she demanded to be returned to her cell. Quinn alternated between cold defiance and cocky bravado. When asked about the chain Matthew wore and her attempt to steal it, she replied, "If I had wanted it, I would have taken it."

At no time did she admit to any wrongdoing, or any responsibility for Matthew's death. I think this is what infuriated my family the most. Even Forslund, the savage monster who had beaten the life out of Matthew, would eventually take responsibility; he apologized at the end of the trial.

The video interviews of Forslund and Quinn would never be seen by the jury. The Crown felt that each of the accused either minimized or denied their involvement, so the jury didn't hear their statements.

Quinn never took any ownership for her part in it, although eyewitness testimony clearly proved she initiated the whole encounter. Later, at the SkyTrain station, she ordered Forslund to finish Matthew, saying, "If you love me—you'll kill him."

The key evidence against Quinn, other than the statements against her made by her own friend, were admissions made during her time in cells. She implicated herself to an undercover police officer, who had been planted to find out what she would admit to, to a fellow con. This evidence is the basis for an appeal that her lawyer has filed, which is pending as I write this account.

The cell plant was placed in cells with Quinn and relayed information to senior investigators after speaking with her.

Quinn made various incriminating comments to the undercover officer, often referring to what she and Forslund had done. At one point, after returning from her interview, she stated, "We're fucked. We're going away for a long time."

The cell plant described not only her statements but her overall attitude and demeanour, which revealed even more about Ms. Quinn's personality. One got the impression from some of her comments that she seemed almost proud of the fact that she and her boyfriend were in jail on murder charges. Taken in context of her personality, that wasn't out of character. Among the "gangsta wanna-bes," a murder charge is the crowning jewel of a criminal lifestyle, bringing a reputation and respect among others in that lifestyle. Her gangster mentality became even more evident later, when we discovered Quinn's Internet site.

Chapter Seventeen

THE GANGSTA WANNA-BE

The strength of a nation
derives from the integrity of the home.

~ Confucius ~

Not only would we be subjected to Quinn inside the courthouse, but we would be tormented by her and her family daily, outside the courthouse. Often, Quinn's friends would come out to support her and they would also glare at us, or try to intimidate witnesses who may have been in court that day to testify. On one of these visits, her girlfriends posed for a photo in front of my entire family, laughing and cackling the entire time. Quinn's own father was the encourager and enabler, taking the photo with his cell phone.

We were devastated to see this amoral and unethical behaviour. They clearly had no respect for our loss. That they would thumb their noses at the gravity of the situation, at Matthew and his family, spoke volumes. These people were from another planet.

It almost seemed that the photograph was some sort of "trophy picture," an impression confirmed when the picture wound up on Katherine Quinn's Nexopia webpage—later that day. This demonstrated, without a shadow of a doubt, how low the entire family was.

Not once did her family try to apologize for their daughter's involvement in Matthew's death. Not once did they show a scintilla of compassion for us.

Just a week or so earlier, I had received a phone call from one of Matthew's friends, telling me that an associate of Quinn's was leaving threatening messages on her Nexopia page. I couldn't figure out how they had found her, but soon realized they had found a memorial page that had been created by Matthew's friends. They were able to send messages to the kids linked to the page. I was sickened by it and did some investigating myself, only to find that Quinn had her own page as well. It was the most disgusting thing I had ever seen!

Throughout the page, she referred to herself as a "Gangsta Bitch," and called her three young children her "pimps." She posted photos of her and the children throwing gangsta hand signs and dressed in gangsta bandannas.

The text on this page gave some insight into the warped mind of Katherine Quinn, who repeatedly referred to those who had testified against her as "rats"; there were vague threats about payback. We later heard in court that this wasn't the first time Quinn had used intimidation. She had been convicted of an assault in 2003 which left the victim requiring twenty stitches. That same victim later filed a complaint against Quinn for uttering threats. Quinn did not contest the allegation and pled guilty. She received no jail time for the offence and was placed on a recognizance.

Quinn posted nasty comments about my family, and even went as far as posting horrific comments about Matthew. David and I contacted the IHIT officers and the Crown prosecutors immediately to notify them of her behaviour. I printed everything off, including the trophy picture and brought it to court with me the following day. We hoped to be able to use the bald evidence of her remorseless attitude to show the judge and the jury just how sick she was.

The media got wind of it that day in court, and the next thing we knew, the pictures and her contemptuous actions were tormenting us on all the newscasts. Our family felt vindicated to see Quinn's true colours exposed.

Quinn was confronted by IHIT and shown the pictures and documents, detailing her late night indiscretions. Her father was in complete shock, as he had no idea that she had taken the photo from his phone and uploaded it onto the Internet for the world to see. When the evidence was brought before Justice Romilly, the defence lawyer, James Millar, lost his mind, and threw another one of his tantrums, stating that my family was interfering with the trial.

The new evidence would not be used against her during the trial, but the Crown suggested that it might be introduced during sentencing. This, however, was not the case, and we all knew it was because Quinn's lawyer would just use its introduction as another excuse for an appeal.

My heart was broken, recognizing that this imbecile was able to walk amongst us, free on bail, thumbing her nose at all concerned, despite breaching her conditions. She not only made a mockery of our justice system, but also of my family, who continued to endure the horrendous details of how Matthew was sacrificed for her thrill kill.

Once again, I felt victimized not only by those who took my child's life, but by the criminal justice system. I had always naïvely believed our system of law and order had been put in place to protect us. But now, I saw the truth—the hard, cold truth.

Her site was finally removed from Nexopia, along with those of her dubious friends who were helping her post her messages. We were grateful. Apparently reports of this blatant abuse of the right to free speech were sent in to the webmaster, who finally removed her page from the site.

Nevertheless, it wasn't the end of it for us. They created message boards on public Internet forums to continue their bashing. They even found Matthew's memorial tribute site, created by a family friend, and had the audacity to begin leaving messages on the site which called me a "media whore." The anonymous cowards remarked that our family was trying to sway the jury by speaking out about the assault on Matthew.

I think the most disturbing excreta they deposited were the postings on public forums—including graphic details of Matthew's murder. They demonstrated total disrespect for a dead child and a grieving family trying vainly to cope with the loss.

I learned more about the Quinns as time progressed; the Brady Bunch they were not. All of the Quinn children seemed to have been in trouble with the law at one time or other. A little over a year before, there had been a B.C.-wide warrant out for the arrest of Quinn's brother for assault with a deadly weapon and uttering threats. I am not certain whether or not he was ever taken into custody because of it.

I later heard through Wendy Dawson that Quinn's mother wanted to send me a message through James Millar; that she wanted me to know she had also lost her own mother to murder.

I don't know why she felt that I should know this. Did she think it would make me feel any better? It didn't. Perhaps she was trying to tell me that she understood my pain. Maybe she felt I would take pity on her. I honestly don't know, but I felt numb—nothing, no sense of sorrow at all for her loss. How could I, when her family had not only taken the life of my innocent son, but was complicit in tormenting the bereaved?

I merely wanted them to feel the pain I was feeling—the pain my family was feeling—but their whole family seemed devoid of "the milk of human kindness."

Chapter Eighteen

BABY ON BOARD—
THE COURTROOM STAFF

*The friend who can be silent with us in a moment of
despair or confusion, who can stay with us in an hour of
grief and bereavement, who can tolerate not knowing...
not healing, not curing...that is a friend who cares.*

~ Henri Nouwen ~

*T*he days that followed were long and draining for us. We tried
everything we could to keep ourselves from falling apart. On many
occasions, other members of our family, or friends, would come and
sit in the courtroom with us to lend their support. Even members of
the public would come and sit for the entire day, hoping to see justice
for Matthew. My family will never forget their compassion, especially
in our darkest days, when we had lost all hope for humanity.

Whenever I was able to come and sit through the trial, I would
bring our young daughter. Since Matthew's murder, I have suffered

terribly from separation anxiety, especially with Chhaya. Because I had almost lost her twice during the pregnancy, I was terrified that something might happen to her. I trusted no one with my children, and even today I continue to struggle with that fear.

David and I would take turns sitting with the baby in the seating area of the courthouse while the other would go into the courtroom. Sometimes my sisters or friends of our family would want a break and they would play with her, so David and I could go in together.

The courthouse is also where I watched Chhaya begin to pull herself up on furniture and start to move her little feet to walk. She was so proud of herself, squealing and smiling at me, but all I could feel was great sadness—my little girl was learning how to walk outside the courtroom where her big brother's accused murderers were being tried. A brother she would never know, a brother who would never get the chance to hold her, play with her, and watch her grow.

We created rituals in order to establish some normalcy in an otherwise very stressful and surreal environment. We would all try to arrive at the New Westminster Courthouse around the same time every morning, buy our coffee or tea, and gather in the second floor seating lounge to sit together and spend a moment chatting.

The Quinn's and their few supporters generally stayed on the first floor until the courtroom was opened. Often our family, friends and supporters would fill our side of Courtroom 208 to capacity. There seemed to be an invisible line down the centre of the courtroom. Quinn's family would sit to the right, with no one crossing the imaginary boundary, other than the media. This was only because most days, there were no more seats available on our side.

If I was not too emotionally spent by the time the morning session ended, we would all have lunch together. We brought our own food from home and, since there were so many of us, we would have a picnic.

The weather most days was cold, so we would take our picnic to the underground parkade, pull out a collapsible camping table and chairs, and eat together. Even though sitting down there was dark and gloomy, smelling faintly of car exhaust, at least it got us away from the stench upstairs. It gave us all a moment to breathe, and get away from the constant hostility coming from the defendants and their cronies. We reviewed anything we had found confusing or overwhelming during the mornings' sessions, or we often changed the topic completely, hoping to clear our minds of all the horrific details of Matthew's assault.

We also carpooled as much as possible, to reduce the individual fuel and parking expenses. My family and our friends were there Monday to Friday, from nine in the morning to five in the evening. We were even brought in on the odd Saturday if Justice Romilly requested it.

The sheriffs responsible for protecting the courthouse came to know us all over the span of the eight-week trial. As we passed through the security checkpoint, they would often smile and ask how things were going, as they performed their searches and screened us.

Chhaya, especially, was a favourite of the female sheriffs. They made a fuss over her, and commented on how cute she was and how well she behaved, as she toddled through the metal detectors, holding my legs to remain standing.

I can never thank all of them enough for the warm smiles that greeted us and the distractions they provided. They brought smiles to our faces even in the darkest of times. They helped in ways they will never know, especially for my sisters, who were present every single day of the trial.

Chapter Nineteen
WITNESSES AND ACCUSED TESTIFY

All that is necessary for the triumph of evil
is that good men do nothing.

~ Edmund Burke ~

Back in Courtroom 208, Crown prosecutor Wendy Dawson would be finishing with the last of the witnesses. The jury heard everyone's version of what they saw and heard that tragic night. One of the young girls who took the stand sobbed uncontrollably as she watched the video footage from the SkyTrain surveillance cameras.

She watched Forslund repeatedly kick and stomp on Matthew, at one point even pulling his tiny body off the cement floor before slamming him back down again. The young witness had to be excused from the courtroom after the video was shown.

"I'm sorry, I'm sorry," she apologized to Crown counsel, Wendy Dawson.

Just earlier in the day, this witness told the jury she was upset by what she saw the night Matthew died. "I saw Rob punching and kicking what I later came to know was Matthew Martins," she testified. "Rob was over Matthew, over his body. Matthew was just lying there, he wasn't doing anything!"

It was hard for us to sit through the witnesses' accounts, as the details were horrific. We also saw the raw pain they were feeling for having seen something so traumatic. It broke our hearts. I wanted nothing more than to reach out to them and hold them in my arms.

We observed as we went through the various stages of the trial that the proceedings in a criminal trial were very closely regulated, and always reverted to the same factor—the rights of the accused. We saw Quinn's defence lawyer, on at least two occasions, try to have a mistrial declared. Of course, that would have been devastating for us, since it meant starting over again.

We had begun to hear that Quinn was going to take the stand. I didn't quite know what to think of it.

On April 4, 2007, in a surprising twist, Katherine Quinn took the stand to deny any responsibility in Matthew's murder. This was a last-minute decision for her, a last-ditch attempt to evade the consequences. James Millar stated that the reason Quinn wanted to take the stand was because she wanted the jury to feel 100% certain that she was not guilty of the crime.

Quinn looked very nervous on the stand as she denied all responsibility for the attack that ended Matthew's life; she even burst into tears when she left the courtroom during a break.

We viewed it as a ploy to try to gain sympathy from the jury, but we sensed that it would boomerang on her—she was hanging herself, up there on the stand.

Listening to Quinn as she testified gave us the distinct impression she had been coached. Her brief statements lacked the emotional content and natural flow of other witnesses. Her speech was very clipped, as if she were saying just enough to answer the questions and no more. On cross examination by the Crown, she was grilled on the inconsistencies in her version of events.

Quinn disputed all the claims of earlier witnesses, saying she did not tell Forslund to kill Matthew. She also denied jumping Matthew to steal his cross necklace. Instead, she said that Matthew had stabbed her and run away.

My family was appalled by her version. We all knew Matthew would never carry a weapon, nor would he ever hurt anyone. It was the stupidest defence she could have dreamed up. How could she think anyone would believe that Matthew, walking all by himself, would—out of the blue—stab some random woman for no reason, while she stood with five other adults in front of her home? Have I mentioned how big Forslund was? That is exactly my point! It never happened. Such transparent lies. Quinn then denied having started the entire assault, even saying that she had seen nothing.

The Last Six Minutes

Quinn's lawyer, James Millar, told the jury Forslund killed Matthew and the evidence they had heard thus far did not establish that Quinn had assisted or encouraged the assault by Forslund. Millar went on to say she never once encouraged Forslund to assault Matthew; nor did she ever utter the words, "If you love me, you will kill him."

We all knew she was committing perjury, but, of course, once again, the victim's family had to sit silently and pray that the jury would see through her lies and recognize the truth.

Matthew's First Christmas – 1988
Matthew was 3 months old, and I was 17

Matthew walking
at 11 months old
Central Park,
Burnaby, BC

Matthew & Mom
Matthew at 12 months &
Mom at 18 years

Aunty Celia & Matthew –
3 years old

Aunty Jeane & Matthew - 3 years old

Danny Martins 7 years old & Matthew Martins 3 years old

My three sons' Braydan (left) Mitchell (Centre) Matthew (Right)
Christmas of 1998

Matthew & Braydan Martins/Summer of 1998

Matthew & Mitchell Martins/ Summer of 1999
Matthew 11 & Mitchell 7

Chhaya at 2 years of age

My three sons' Trout Lake-Vancouver, BC

Mitchell & Matthew Martins/ Ages 7 & 11
Best Buddies

Matthew on our Wedding Day, August 2001

Matthew with Mom & Step Dad David 2000

Matthew Martins at 13 years old, standing by our bay window

Danny Martins & Matthew Martins (Cousins) Thanksgiving of 2003

Matthew & his baby cousin MaKayla Motz, Thanksgiving 2003

The last photos I took of Matthew before he was murdered
2005

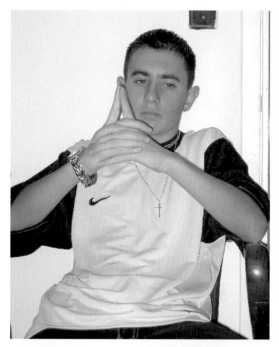

Matthew Martins 2005

Matthew Martins 2005

Matthew Martins 2005

Memorial Erected on the site of his Murder the following Day
July 3, 2005
(The date on the photograph is incorrect)
The site remained for over two weeks, and grew in size at an hourly rate

Matthew's Final Resting Place

Our family still celebrates Matthew's Birthday; he would have been 20 years old
September 20th, 2008.

Chapter Twenty
ANOTHER LOSS

Any man can be a father,
but it takes someone special to be a dad.
~ Anne Geddes ~

*J*ust five days after Quinn took the stand, my family was dealt another hard blow. Our father, Louçiano Martins, passed away suddenly on April 9th, 2007. Our pillar of strength and the man we adored lost his life to pancreatic cancer. My sisters and I never even knew our father had cancer until it was too late.

I had applied to the Victim Safety Unit weeks before the trial started, in hopes of getting financial aid to have my father brought to Canada. David and I couldn't afford the expense, as I had not returned to work—we were still struggling to make ends meet. I needed my dad more than ever, and all I could think of was crawling into his lap like I had as a young child, just to be close to him. I needed his comfort and his strength to get me through the trial. Not even two weeks later, I received a letter in the mail telling me that the application had been denied, as my father was not considered an immediate family member.

I was infuriated by the refusal, and couldn't believe they would deny my family this request. At this point I had already discovered that the government agencies and resources that were supposed to be in place for the victims and their families constituted nothing more than a farce. It seemed that I had to beg for any little thing, and even then, I was told I did not qualify.

Once I had cried myself out and calmed myself down, I called the office and spoke to one of the victims' services workers. I was extremely lucky to reach a young woman who was very sympathetic and understanding. She told me to appeal the application by writing a letter explaining that my father had helped raise Matthew the first few years of his life. As hard as it was for me, I sat down and wrote about the relationship my father had with his grandson, and the important role he had played in my child's life.

It would be another week before we would receive news that our request to have our father, who was living in Portugal, brought to Canada, was granted. I called my sisters immediately to tell them the news. I also called the worker who had helped us and thanked her for all she had done to help make this happen. I have thought many times since that day that, if it had been another worker, perhaps I would never have known that the original refusal could be appealed. How many other families would never know they had these options?

I still remember the day he arrived. My sister and I arrived at the airport with a few friends of the family, to meet him. We paced back and forth, watching the monitors above the terminal, in hopes of catching a glimpse of him before he reached the final set of doors. It seemed like forever before we caught a glimpse of our dad. Before he could even get out the sliding doors, my sister Jeane and I dove under the barricades and ran as fast as we could towards him. As we rushed up the corridor, we nearly took out a few other passengers in our excitement and we almost knocked our father's luggage right off his cart. We held him so tightly and cried tears of pain for Matthew and tears for the years we had lost while our father had lived abroad.

We began to suspect our father was ill, but we had no idea it was cancer. We chalked it up to the stress from the trial, and a terrible bout of the flu he had had just weeks prior. We noticed he had lost a significant amount of weight and seemed very tired, but because he never complained about anything, we had no idea. David and I bought cases of Ensure meal supplements for him in hopes that he would regain some strength, but he just seemed to get weaker as the days progressed.

My father never believed in seeing doctors—I guess it was just the way he had always been. I honestly can't recall ever seeing my father seek medical attention for anything. He always had his own methods of relieving pain with old natural remedies from the old country.

Dad eventually told us that he thought it might be a good idea if he returned home to see a doctor, as he wasn't insured here in

Canada. I began making the arrangements to change his flight, and he made his way back home at the end of March.

We received a call from my father's wife Cidalia a few days later to let us know that he had a very high fever, and that she was taking him to the nearest hospital in Faro. She called us again the next day to tell us that they had done some tests, and had diagnosed our father with pancreatic cancer. It was in the very late stages. The doctors could only try to make him as comfortable as possible.

My father, at sixty-four years of age, would be the last of the Martins, as he had never sired any sons to carry on the family name. This was exactly why I had given my firstborn son my maiden name at birth. I wanted my father's last name to be carried on, but those dreams were shattered when Forslund and Quinn murdered my son.

Regardless of my father's death, the trial continued. My sisters and I took a few days away from the trial to mourn our father's passing and to prepare for his funeral in his home town in Portugal.

Jeane, the eldest of the four girls, and our cousin, Jose, would be the only ones flying out to be there for our father's funeral. Sally, Tina and I prepared to have a service here for our father.

The strangest thing, though, was that I had an inkling this was going to happen. I think that I was somehow sent a sign or a message so I could brace myself and prepare for the sudden loss of yet another important person in my life.

Chapter Twenty-One

DREAMS: ATTORNEYS FOR THE DEFENCE

Live as brave men; and if fortune is adverse,
front its blows with brave hearts.

~ Cicero ~

*T*hree weeks before my father passed away, I was suddenly rocked awake by a terrible dream. Every word of this dream was vivid and clear. For some reason, I couldn't shake it. As soon as I could, I called my sisters to tell them about it. I cannot remember if I called Sally or Jeane first, but this is what I told them about that very lucid dream.

I began by telling my sister that I had dreamt that I was standing in complete darkness. It was so dark that not only could I not see in front of me, but I could not even see my own body or hands. I stood there a few moments terribly afraid—until I suddenly heard Matthew's voice. I was startled to hear his voice. In my dream I knew he had passed away; I had not heard the sound of his voice in so long. I would hear Matthew say in a very calm voice, "Mom." I began to cry out for him, and I pleaded for him to let me see him, but nothing—I remained in darkness.

I realized that the more I cried for him, the quieter he became, so I quickly calmed myself so that I could hear him. I felt a calmness surround me as Matthew began to speak. He told me, "Mom, DeDe is coming to visit me really soon." Matthew and the other grandchildren had always called my father DeDe, their nickname for him. It took me a moment to understand and process what he was saying about his grandfather. I responded that I didn't think that was possible because his grandfather was too young—it was not his time yet. He then said, "Mom, you need to help him." And then, "Mom—it's too late."

I continued to tell him that I didn't know what to do, and that I was scared. Slowly his voice became more difficult to hear, drifting farther and farther away until once again I stood in absolute silence and darkness.

I began to yell his name over and over, pleading for him to come back to me, telling him I was afraid to be alone in the dark without him, only to be ripped awake and brought back to reality.

Looking back now, it all seems so surreal. I wondered why this was all happening. I kept asking myself what I had ever done in my life to deserve such terrible pain. I think the only comfort I could take from the loss of my father was that my father was now with Matthew, and they would be together. At that point I needed something to cling to, to keep me from going off the deep end.

My sisters and I did all we could to support each other through yet another devastating loss, during the long days in the latter part of the trial. We all knew that Wendy Dawson was wrapping up her arguments for the prosecution. Soon it would be the defence's turn to make their case.

We were all dreading having to listen to Mr. Millar's and Ms. Bastow's interpretations of what happened that tragic night, but we also knew that this was how it was done.

They would try to persuade the jury of their clients' innocence, in itself a great insult. I feared how they would try to paint a picture of Matthew as a bad kid, or a trouble maker. To think they would try to say that Matthew had done something to deserve his fate made my blood boil. We had to prepare ourselves for the unthinkable.

The great part was that they couldn't do it; Matthew had never been in any trouble with the law. Matthew had always been the one who was picked on or bullied, his entire life, due to his size. Regardless, we were prepared to watch Mr. Millar put on a show in the courtroom, and he didn't disappoint. I remember looking over at the jury a few times during one of his flamboyant rants and noticed we weren't the only ones who were convinced that the man had lost his mind. I wondered if they too would mimic his ridiculous antics later, behind closed doors. I saw it throughout the trial—someone would mimic his mannerisms and speak as he did, accentuating his every word to make us all laugh. I think it was a way for those present to release some tension. I think by this point, Quinn's behaviour outside and inside the courthouse appeared to have worn Millar's patience thin.

It began to show even to those sitting quietly, observing from the sidelines. When you are in close proximity for long periods of time, you begin to pick up on others' mannerisms and quirks. Watching others was something my husband David, had done for years. He is an internal investigator for a major retail chain—it comes with the territory. He would sit back quietly and observe their every move, the manner in which they spoke, walked, and stood.

Our bodies react to situations: to someone who can read body language, minute details telegraphed Millar's frustration. This was a man who didn't like to lose. We were all very aware of this.

I don't know how that man could sleep at night; I don't know how any criminal defence attorney who makes his living defending evil monsters such as Quinn and Forslund could sleep at night. It is one thing to defend someone if he is really innocent of the crime, but there was nothing in these circumstances that suggested innocence. Karen Bastow's cross examinations were extremely boring. I think by this point, she and Forslund had realized the jig was up—they didn't have a leg to stand on. For the duration of the trial, she sat quietly in her chair, only asking a witness a question here and there.

Of course, this did not relax us much, as we knew the days to come would begin with both parties' closing arguments, and from what I could gather this wasn't going to be easy.

Chapter Twenty-Two

TOLL ON THE FAMILY: THERAPY

When you lose someone you love, you die too, and
you wait around for your body to catch up.

~ John Scalzi, *Old Man's War* ~

*A*t this point in the trial, it had been almost two years since Matthew's murder, and I was still suffering terribly from the loss. I continued to be plagued with night terrors, and moments of complete despair. I couldn't imagine living the rest of my days without my child. As the days went by, my heart filled with an even greater sadness. My boys were also struggling with their pain, but often children don't know how to express their feelings. Sometimes their pain was communicated in different ways.

Mitchell had withdrawn into his own dark silence and rarely spoke to anyone about what he was feeling. He was filled with a hatred for the world; sometimes my husband and I would be the ones to take the brunt of his anger, as we were the ones closest to him. I sometimes felt as though he blamed us for what had happened to his brother. Weren't we the parents, the ones who are supposed to keep them safe? As a mother it was my responsibility to keep them safe and away from harm; in his eyes I had failed miserably. Knowing it caused me unbearable pain. I had no idea how I was going to help him.

They will never be the same children they once were. Their childhood—their innocence—was stolen from them; they suffered terrible guilt for enjoying anything in their lives. Mitchell has battled bouts of depression so severe he can barely get out of bed to get to school.

As parents, David and I are doing everything we can to help them get through this by providing them with all the necessary tools and resources out there. We can only pray that our children will find something in their lives that will bring them happiness. When they feel as though they can no longer bear the weight of their brother's death, I remind them of how loved they are, and of how proud Matthew would be of them today.

All I ask is that they don't give up on themselves. I want them to live their lives as best they can, and to never forget how much their big brother loved and adored them. Both my boys have probably had more therapy these past few years than most people would in a lifetime. What they have suffered and endured would bring most grown men to their knees.

David and I also sought professional help, especially in the first few months after Matthew's death. I was having terrible fits of rage, and I didn't know how to cope with the vivid images that continued to play in my head. During the first few months after Matthew's murder, we weren't given many details. More likely, my family felt it best that I not know the extent of the beating he took that night, but my brain would try to piece together whatever information I did have, with images and sounds that my imagination concocted to try to fill the gaps. It was awful; it was worse than awful, but unfortunately there are no words to accurately describe my feelings. I really felt as though I were losing my mind.

I remember lying on my bed, staring at the ceiling, imagining how I could hurt Quinn and Forslund for what they had done. I saw myself doing horrific things to Quinn's children while she was made to watch. The moment I had this vision or fantasy or whatever it is called, I sprang up and vomited all over myself and the bed. How could I have even thought of such a disgusting thing? I was beside myself and knew I needed some professional help, right away.

We were very fortunate to have therapy provided to us through my husband's employer. We didn't go through Victims' Services for the allotted counselling visits they offered us and looking back now, I'm glad we didn't. I've watched many families go through hell trying to obtain counselling, as the doctors they chose were declined due to the cost of their sessions. Who can put a time limit or a price on that type of therapeutic help? It is absolutely insane!

David and I decided to visit a therapist in downtown Vancouver a few days later, and I was stunned by the outcome. As I recounted our tragic loss, and everything I was feeling, I began to hear sobbing. I looked up to see that the person who was supposed to be listening to my cries of pain—was crying herself. I didn't know what to do, or how to feel about this display of emotion from a medical professional.

I looked over at David who seemed to be a little confused as well. I stammered through the rest of my appointment, telling her in graphic detail the nature of my horrific daydreams. She began by blowing her nose, telling me that I was not crazy, that thoughts like mine were, of course, a natural and normal means for me to cope with what we had been through. The only difference was that I knew that I was never going to follow through on such a horrific act of violence. I was thankful to hear her tell me I wasn't going to turn into some kind of crazy killer; after our appointment, that scene never played out in my head again.

I never did return to her office again, but replaced her with a team of psychiatrists and therapists through my family doctor, and my OB-GYN. I needed to have as much support for the duration of my pregnancy as possible, and I wanted to be monitored for any signs of postpartum depression once our daughter was born. I would take no chances with my children's lives, and David and I set about educating ourselves about the condition so we'd be able to see the signs, should any appear.

Chapter Twenty-Three

CLOSING ARGUMENTS

Liberty, equality—bad principles!
The only true principle for humanity is justice; and
justice to the feeble is protection and kindness.

~ Henri-Frédéric Amiel ~

On April 11th, 2008, the Crown and the defence began their closing arguments. The courtroom was packed on that day, and those in attendance included the Crown prosecutors' family members, media, and other lawyers curious to hear the closing arguments in what had become a very high profile case. Although I can't remember who presented first, I will summarize the highlights of their arguments.

We were riveted to our seats for the duration, awed by Wendy Dawson's compelling presentation of the facts. Wendy began by thanking the jury members for the time and attention they had given throughout the trial. She asked that they give serious consideration to the evidence, and reminded them of their duty to judge the case dispassionately and without sympathy for Matthew, Katherine Quinn or Robert Forslund.

She went over the main points of the crime, pointing out the many inconsistencies and blatant contradictions in Quinn's testimony. Wendy highlighted Forslund's deliberate intention to cause death; he had demonstrated foresight during the violent act when he paused in his actions several times to demand ID from witnesses. He briefly ceased the assault to go and speak to Quinn and inquire about her condition, then returned with a beer bottle to slit Matthew's throat. This would prove—beyond a doubt—that he had the intent to kill Matthew. Forslund's professed guilt and remorse paled in comparison to the savagery of his crime.

Wendy reminded the judge and the jury of the unspeakable and sadistic violence of this offence. She stated that Forslund's attempt to plead guilty to manslaughter only emphasized that Forslund wasn't willing to face up to the full effect of his culpability in this most brutal murder.

She began by touching upon the testimonies of the four key witnesses, and the evidence of the SkyTrain video. She acknowledged that although the case had been dramatic, the jury members must go into the deliberation room with their native common sense and a dose of reality.

122

She repeatedly reminded the jury of the evidence before them, and that they could, at any time during their deliberations, watch the footage from the SkyTrain station. She noted, however, that she hoped they wouldn't have to. The words, "Beyond all reasonable doubt," were mentioned a few times throughout her argument.

Karen Bastow's defence of Forslund was concise. She began by stating that Forslund didn't deny beating Matthew that night. Bastow reminded the jury that he had tried to plead guilty to a lesser charge of manslaughter, but the Crown had refused to accept the plea. Bastow stated that the Crown would "...urge you, the jury to convict on the charge of murder..." She pleaded with the jury to find Forslund, instead, guilty of manslaughter. Her reasons were twofold. First, Forslund's mental state was affected by the fact that he was drinking. Evidence indicated he drank approximately twelve beers over a seven hour period. Although his blood alcohol level had not been medically measured at the time, common sense would suggest that he was impaired. She asserted that it was also common sense to infer that the alcohol impaired his judgment.

While Bastow offered his "drunkenness" as a mitigating factor for the murder, we noted in the testimony that he was not so impaired that he couldn't drive the car from the SkyTrain Station to Surrey Memorial Hospital.

Second, she pointed out that Forslund was provoked into action by the belief that Matthew had stabbed Quinn. Provocation has, in previous cases, been used to reduce the intent of murder to manslaughter; she cited case law to support her statement. Bastow closed by stating that the burden of proof is on the Crown. It was their duty to prove intent in a murder charge.

James Millar reminded the jury that they must use the law to judge innocence or guilt in a criminal case. The standard was absolute proof, not reasonable doubt. "Standards," he said, "are set high because mistakes are made, and we don't want to send an innocent to jail. The jury must keep an open mind; one's truth is another's lie."

We all thought this was ironic coming from a defence lawyer, who bases much of his career on other people's lies and denials.

Millar lectured the jury regarding the different accounts they had heard from witnesses. He stated that what the jury must consider was the assumption of innocence. He shone a harsh spotlight on the slight inconsistencies between witnesses' statements; he told the jury that if any doubt existed, they must give credit to the accused. Millar called the witnesses unreliable, and suggested they had been influenced by police officers. He cited an example of a police investigator telling one of the young female witnesses, "You have to do the right thing, and put these two away."

Millar's biggest issue throughout the entire trial and his basis for the now-pending appeal would be the use of the cell plant evidence. He repeatedly stated that undercover evidence needed to be thrown out, as he felt it was a scheme by police to pin this crime on Quinn. He believed that the evidence from the cell plant was unreliable, since the alleged incriminating conversation had not been recorded.

Millar suggested the there had been no recording because of some sinister purpose on the part of the police investigators. The explanation we were given was that there simply hadn't been enough time to wire the cell with covert surveillance. The plant had been sent in cold, for fear that Quinn would be released soon. Mr. Millar urged the jury to find his client "Miss Quinn," innocent of the charge.

Chapter Twenty-Four
THE JURY RETIRES; THE VERDICT

Let the punishment match the offence.

~ Marcus Tullius Cicero ~

*T*he jury went out to deliberate on Thursday, April 12th, 2007 at four-twenty-five in the afternoon. We were told at around nine-thirty that evening that they would continue their deliberations the next morning. We sat in the seating areas of the New Westminster Courthouse for what seemed like an eternity. We arrived at nine in the morning, and waited there until almost ten o'clock at night the following day as well. When we did go home, there was little sleep. David and I paced around the house in the dark, staring out the bay window of our home in silence. We didn't know what to think, or even what we should be expecting; the waiting was excruciating. Every second on the clock seemed like an eternity.

The Last Six Minutes

At the courthouse, our friends and family did what they could to help ease the time. My aunt and uncle brought boxes of strawberries and cookies, and we ate out of sheer boredom and anxiety. Chhaya entertained everyone with her silliness, giving us all a reason to smile and laugh a little amidst the deadening stress.

Card games sprang up on coffee tables and a chess board appeared. We all shared each other's company. The crowd waiting for the outcome fluctuated in size, as some had to leave to go to work, pick up their kids, go home for a shower, and so on.

After almost two-and-a-half days of waiting, we were finally told the jury had reached a decision in their deliberations. The verdict finally came back just after lunch on Saturday, April 14th, 2007. We scrambled to get everyone in the family back to the courthouse, frantically calling my cousins and those who wanted to be notified. Even the media had spent most of the past two days with us. Others would arrive just in the nick of time.

The rush of people through the main doors caused a human traffic jam; the sheriffs couldn't seem to get us past the security check fast enough. Pockets were emptied as quickly as possible into the trays provided; wands beeped furiously at the forgotten items in our pockets. I couldn't seem to think straight; every moment of the last four weeks flashed before my eyes. It was finally going to be over, and all I would continue to say in my head over and over again was, "Please, God—have mercy on us!"

The fate of Forslund and Quinn was about to be played out right in front of us, and we could only pray that the jury members had made the right decision. It was always so hard to read them, or gauge their thoughts throughout the trial as they always sat almost motionless and expressionless in their seats. A few would cry, or glare at the accused once in awhile, but that could have meant anything, really. We could only hope that they would see past all the smoke and mirrors created by the defence.

On this day, I had decided to bring an eight-by-ten photo of Matthew with me to the courthouse. I needed the comfort and his presence with me. As we all rushed to take our seats in the courtroom, the tension was high; you could feel it. We rose as Justice Romilly entered the room, and watched as the sheriffs brought Forslund in from the side door. They placed him back into the prisoner's dock where he had sat for the past few weeks. We overheard Bastow tell the sheriffs in a low voice they should be prepared to restrain Forslund if the verdict went against Quinn.

Quinn walked in on her own accord with her father close behind. Quinn was also placed in the prisoner's dock, next to Forslund's. Quinn's father was the only one present in court from the defendant's side that day, while my family, our friends, and Matthew's friends packed the room.

The jury finally entered the room. I remember looking at each and every one of their faces as they were seating themselves. I couldn't read what they were thinking; I wished that David was sitting next to me at this point. David had stayed out in the hallway with our daughter as she was too little to be in the room with us. One of the sheriffs had his ear to the door to give David a play-by-play of what was transpiring in Room 208.

The benches we sat on were overflowing, and the family members on the end had to swing sideways in order to sit comfortably. You could feel the bench vibrating beneath us from the nerve-induced teeth-chattering, the anxiety and stress we were feeling in anticipation of the jury's decisions.

Justice Romilly addressed the court and informed the clerk that they would begin with the jury's decision on Forslund.

I can't really remember what either Justice Romilly or the court clerks said because my eyes were glued on the jury members. Matthew's photo sat upright on my lap facing the court, my left arm looped through my cousin Jose's.

The jury members were asked what verdict they had decided on to the charge of second degree murder for Robert Forslund. I held my breath; the jury foreman stood and said, "Guilty." All twelve of them had found Forslund guilty beyond all reasonable doubt on the charge of murdering my little boy.

A huge sigh was heard in unison from the packed benches. Forslund's head fell forward at that moment. It felt good to see this disheartened reaction from him. The bastard!

Quinn's turn was much different. We really had no idea what to expect. I think our anxiety was exacerbated due to her tormenting us terribly during the entire court process. I have never hated anyone the way I hated them, but she took first place, even ahead of Forslund. I don't know about the others, but I had completely stopped breathing at this point. My body shook violently while I waited what seemed like an eternity for the jurists to deliver their verdict.

The jury foreman was again asked by Justice Romilly if they had come to a verdict on the charge of second degree murder for Katherine Quinn. His response again: "Guilty."

Quinn's lawyer immediately requested a poll of the jurists. Jurists are rarely polled unless the jury is "hung," that is, split; or if a narrow majority of the panel has won the decision.

One by one, they stood and said, "Guilty," "Guilty,"... "GUILTY!!!" All twelve unanimously agreed.

The courtroom erupted with screams and cheers by my family members and those present who had sat through the entire trial. My sister, Sally, rushed into the courtroom at that very moment. She had heard the screams as she ran up the stairs towards the courtroom, and couldn't understand what had just happened. My nephew Danny was just a few steps ahead of her in the stairwell. They both lurched forward as fast as they could towards the entrance of Room 208. Sally's hair was still wet; she had been pulled out of the shower by her husband when they received the urgent call to get back to the courthouse for the verdicts. Danny wedged himself next to me and grabbed my hand in his. I will never forget thinking to myself as he sat there in his dirty work clothes, looking into my eyes, how much he reminded me of Matthew. Danny is just a few years older than Matthew, but you could have sworn they were brothers; the resemblance was striking.

Quinn burst into tears, and screamed over us to her father sitting behind our group. I watched her closely and heard her ask her father to help her. She told him that she loved him.

WHAT?? This monster actually felt something? Quinn then looked over at Forslund and yelled, "You told me this wouldn't happen!"

I was dumbfounded by this comment. She honestly thought she was going to get away with murder. I felt euphoric watching her and her father in turmoil. I experienced such a rush of emotions, but the one that overwhelmed me was vindication.

I watched as the sheriffs placed her in handcuffs, bawling her eyes out. She was still trying to reach out to her father.

Chapter Twenty- Five
PREPARING MY VICTIM
IMPACT STATEMENT

They say that time heals all wounds
but all it's done so far is give me more time
to think about how much I miss you.

~ Ezbeth Wilder ~

*W*e received a call from the Crown prosecutor's office to let us know that sentencing would be on April 27th, 2007; just two weeks after the verdicts had come in. I was surprised that Justice Romilly had come to a decision so quickly, as Wendy had warned us it could take some time.

I had been preparing my "victim impact statement" in weeks prior and would finally get the chance to read it before the court. I think the only thing that bothered me was that, even before I got my chance to read it, the accused and their defence lawyers would already have read it themselves. It bothered me to think that if I had written anything outside the guidelines I had been instructed to use, it would have been removed from my statement. The fact that it is *verboten* to say or suggest personal opinions on how the courts should rule is extremely hard. All you are allowed to discuss is how the crime affected you emotionally, physically and financially.

I can see why many victims and their families choose not to write statements. You almost feel like it's not worth re-opening the wounds. I chose to write one. I needed both Forslund and Quinn to hear how they had destroyed my family's life. I knew that I could write a very powerful statement even in my darkest moments. Even with the restrictions, I appreciated being given the chance to stand just feet away from my son's killers to read it.

The courtroom was packed on the day of sentencing and the back doors were kept open to allow everyone present to hear what went on. The reporters were placed in the now-vacant jury box to better hear and see what was happening. Quinn had four people there to support her; Matthew's supporters and our family numbered in the dozens. Forslund never had any family or friends present to support him through the court process. We had been told that Forslund was from Manitoba, raised by alcoholic parents. He had lived in foster homes for most of his childhood. It didn't surprise us to see that no one ever showed up for the trial to support him, nor did we feel any pity for his isolation.

The Crown and the defence would address Justice Romilly with their sentencing suggestions in the first part of the morning session. At this point, Wendy Dawson had Sergeant Ross, from the IHIT team, come in and attempt to enter into the record the evidence we had accumulated of Quinn's nefarious website activity. They hoped that her on-line swaggering, bravado, taunts and threats against witnesses and our family would be considered in part of the judge's sentencing. Unfortunately, Justice Romilly declined to have these documents entered, perhaps having already observed enough through Quinn's testimony and behaviour at trial to ascertain her true character. The on-line part of Quinn's life, although now in the public domain, would not be used against her in court.

The sentencing submissions began, and Wendy Dawson's request with respect to Forslund was a sentence of life imprisonment with no possibility for parole for twenty years. For Quinn, Wendy submitted that her sentence should also be life imprisonment, with no possibility for parole for at least twelve to fourteen years. Although Quinn was no stranger to the law, her criminal record was not as extensive as Forslund's. Wendy sought a lesser sentence to reflect her criminal past.

Although she didn't physically cause the injuries that killed Matthew, she provoked the initial assault, and gave the order to Forslund to finish him off. It could then be argued that giving the order made her even more culpable than Forslund, who was merely the mechanism. However, as we were informed, the law doesn't see it that simply.

The Crown reminded the court of Forslund's twenty previous convictions, two of them violent. One was a robbery, for which he was sentenced to eighteen months imprisonment in 1996; the other conviction was for a motor vehicle offence where, at seventeen years of age, he forced a police cruiser off the road, resulting in injuries to the officers. For this violent offence he was sentenced to a paltry one year in jail.

As we sat listening, all of us wondered why this guy had ever been released back into the community. Forslund was a walking time bomb, just waiting to go off, and if it hadn't been my son that night, it would have eventually been someone else.

Forslund's defence counsel began by reminding the court that even before the trial had begun, he had agreed to plead guilty to manslaughter, but the Crown had refused to accept that proposal. She asked that the parole ineligibility for him fall within the ten-to-fifteen year range.

Karen Bastow asked that the following mitigating factors be considered as well: Forslund was drunk at the time of the offence, and he had shown remorse by offering to plead guilty to manslaughter at the early stages of the proceedings. Bastow also stated that at the time of the murder, he was under the impression that his girlfriend had been seriously stabbed by Matthew, and suggested that this might have provided some degree of provocation. Further, she reminded the court that there was a substantial five-year gap in Forslund's criminal record at the time of the offence.

I can't express how much it hurt to hear them accuse Matthew of stabbing Quinn, especially since it was never proven. I know it never happened. The doctors who had examined Quinn in the emergency ward—had they lied on the stand? What would they have had to

136

gain? They clearly stated that it was an abrasion, an excoriation of the skin which could have been caused during the struggle by anything, including a zipper on Matthew's clothing, his watch band, a button—anything. It required nothing more than a bandage.

It made me so angry that Matthew wasn't even here to defend himself, and they kept coming back to it as if it justified them murdering my son—because of an accidental scratch.

Bastow would also state that Forslund had apologized for murdering my son, but I can honestly tell you that it meant nothing to us. I don't think either of them was ever sincerely sorry. The only thing they regretted was getting caught.

Quinn's counsel, James Millar stated that there would be no reason to depart from the general rule of ten years, and he thought five to seven years was more appropriate. His reason for this leniency? Quinn had a very close relationship with her family, and her absence would have a devastating effect on them.

Close family? Don't make me laugh. We learned that she was estranged from her ex-husband and Social Services had removed her children from her care prior to this sordid incident with Matthew. After the second week of the trial, even her mother no longer made it to court anymore, only her father.

He then mentioned that Quinn had also lost a family member to murder, and understood what my family was going through. I don't think she could understand anything outside her small sphere of animal desires, let alone the pain of losing a child by murder. Had she been affected at all at by the loss of her family member, her life shouldn't have turned out the way it had. Quinn was, in my opinion, a sick bitch—no different than any other run-of-the-mill psychopath.

Once all the parties had made their sentencing submissions, Justice Romilly called for a break. The courtroom was so full of people that morning that I was beginning to feel a bit nauseous from the heat. I was also nervous about reading my statement before Justice Romilly and Matthew's murderers. I decided to take Chhaya outside for some fresh air, and give myself a moment to gather my thoughts.

As I exited the building with the baby bundled in my arms, I noticed Quinn's brother standing to my right about ten feet away. I heard him yelling, but it took me a moment to realize it was me he was yelling at. I looked behind me just to make sure, and sure enough there was no one there. I tightened my hold on Chhaya, not sure what this maniac was about to do. I looked through the tinted windows into the courthouse to see if I could catch the attention of one of the sheriffs. As soon as I turned my face back towards Quinn's brother, he began to yell again. Every second word was a profanity, with his hands waving like a crazy person. Perhaps it was mostly his gangsta wanna-be swagger that I found repulsive. I noticed he had two black eyes, and it didn't take a brain surgeon at that point to figure out why. He was telling me I should come to Surrey so he could kick the fucking shit right out of me. His friend standing next to him began calling me a media whore, and claimed that I had swayed the jury because I had a big mouth, and had spoken to the press.

At this point, I had had more than enough. I couldn't believe this was happening to me with the baby in my arms. This family had no respect or shame! The sheriffs had finally noticed what was happening and came outside to bring me back in safely. Quinn's brother was removed from the courthouse immediately; this had not been the first time this had happened since the trial began.

I told the sheriff what had happened, and I was asked not to leave the building again without them or David. Members of the IHIT team escorted us to the car at the end of the day. I just couldn't wait for all of it to be over. I had endured enough pain and torment to last a lifetime.

Chapter Twenty-Six
MY TURN—ARTICULATING THE LOSS

So long as little children are allowed to suffer,
there is no true love in this world.

~ Isodora Duncan ~

*W*e returned to the courtroom after the first break. Once Justice
Romilly had entered and everyone had settled, Wendy came to get
me from my seat. She led me to the witness stand. I felt a rush of heat
envelop me; I wasn't sure if I was going to be able to do this. I could
feel the murderers' eyes on me; I began to shake uncontrollably. I was
instantly overwhelmed by every emotion possible at that moment—
anger, sorrow, fear and all the others mixed into one.

As I took a deep breath to try to calm myself and focus, I tried
to force myself to look over at Forslund sitting to my right, but I
could not. I was too afraid to see his face. I was afraid that I would
see the last thing my son had seen before he was killed. I was only
able to look down to my right where Wendy was seated at a table

and directly ahead of me where the reporters were seated in the jury box.

I began to read my statement, hoping that everyone could hear me. I was overcome with tears of pain even before I had reached the end of the first paragraph. This was how it read:

I cannot even begin to describe the emotional pain I have endured since the loss of my beautiful son, Matthew. There are no words to explain the pain that emanates from my soul. My life, as I knew it, ended on the morning of July 2nd, 2005, when I had to say goodbye forever to my sixteen-year-old son. I would not even get the chance to kiss his beautiful face, or even look into those eyes, as he was covered with blood-soaked towels.

The only thing I was given to hold were his hands, and even so, the stench of his blood that had seeped into his skin and fingernails remains with me always. Watching my son take his last breath was the most terrifying moment of my life, I wanted it to be me, not this child who had so much to give back to this world, who had so much love to give.

This is my last memory of him before he passed on. Leaving my son's body at the hospital, and not even getting any of his belongings only exacerbated the situation for me. Not a single item of clothing, jewellery, wallet—nothing was left for me to hold on to. Driving home from the hospital that day was the longest drive of my life, I knew that his two younger brothers would be anxiously waiting to see their brother coming home with us, with some stitches and cuts, but no, I was left tell them that their brother had succumbed to the brutal assault to his brain and body. I watched his siblings go from being happy little boys, to angry ones, in a matter of hours. Standing in the shower screaming their brother's name, asking God why? What had they done to deserve this?

For the first 6 months after Matthew passed away, my mind would actually try and tell me that it was a mistake, that the boy who died was not actually my son. I fought hard to repress these feelings, sitting by the bay window of our home, waiting, watching for Matthew to come home as I usually did before his death. It wasn't until I realized that the reason I was feeling this was because I never got to see his face, not even during his funeral, as the damages to his head/face were too severe. I truly felt as though I were losing my mind, I really believed he was going to come through the front door. I have since been able to grasp that he is gone, but I will never be okay with it—never.

Matthew's younger siblings' lives will forever be changed. Nothing will ever give them pleasure, as they tend to have guilt, guilt for having a moment of happiness, when their big brother will never have any of it. It has taken me over a year to even allow my children the luxury of having any kind of social lives. I'm afraid that something will happen to them, afraid someone will hurt them, or even worse—kill them. I have become a hovering mother, who must be in constant contact with my children. If they are even five minutes late coming in from school, I begin to panic, and have anxiety. My mind starts to think of the most horrible things and I'm ready to call the police over every little thing. This of course has taken a toll on my relationship with the boys, as they don't understand why they are being punished for being late after school, or for wanting to go visit their friends.

The impact this has had on Matthew's two younger brothers has been severe. Braydan was just nine at the time of Matthew's death, and has had to try and deal with the pain in his own little way. He has shown his grief by becoming defiant, and angry at the adults around him. He has had to be removed from the only school he has ever known, due to his inability to focus on his academics. His teachers have informed me that he had begun signing his work, and the school sign in sheets as Matthew Martins. When asked why he had done this, he stated that he wanted to live his life as Matthew, and didn't want for anyone to forget his brother. He even went as far as to dress exactly as Matthew would in hopes of preserving his brother's memory in his own little way. Braydan has also kept Matthew's shoes at the end of his bed since this happened, and every once in awhile he will slip them on, trying to be close to his brother, he also sleeps in his brother's shirts, and has asked that I not wash them, as he finds comfort in the clothing smelling like his big brother.

He has had to have weekly visits to a child psychologist, to try and get through his grief with "play therapy." Braydan will now be moved again for the third time since this all happened to the Alderwood Program, a school for children who need constant therapeutic and psychiatric care. I can only pray that he will find some inner strength to get through all of this, but as a mother, I fear that this pain will indeed last for what should be the most carefree, wonderful years of his life. He also carries a little framed photo of his brother wherever he goes. He keeps this in his pocket as a little reminder that Matthew is with him.

Mitchell, who was just days away from his 13th birthday, will forever be reminded of his brother's death, at a time when he should be celebrating. Mitchell has not been well since this happened, and now suffers with terrible anxiety and depression. Since his brother's death, he has begun sleeping with his bedroom lights on, and has left school due to bouts of anxiety and not wanting to leave the house. We continue to try and find Mitchell resources to help, but his reluctance to discuss his problems with others has made it difficult. Mitchell now sleeps in Matthew's room so that he can feel closer to him, all of Matthew's pictures and posters just where he had left them. Many nights I hear Mitchell crying himself to sleep, and all I can do is hold him, and comfort him. He cries out in pain for his brother to come back, but I can never bring his brother back, or change the events of that horrible night.

When Matthew was killed, I was in the first trimester of my pregnancy. I fought so hard to try and keep strong, but the shock and stress of it all would eventually challenge the life of my unborn child also. At twenty-seven weeks I was under complete bed rest due to premature labour, and bleeding.

I was sent into an even greater depression, afraid I was going to have to endure the loss of another child. This pregnancy and my family were the only thing keeping me together through all of this, and I knew that if I lost this baby, it would, for certain, be my demise. The thought of Matthew not being able to hold or meet his new baby sister caused me so much grief and angst. It was as though I was constantly being tortured every second of the day and night. The boys had begun suppressing their sadness as they saw how this affected me on a daily bases. They would hide and cry, or lash out at others in anger; they no longer trusted the adults around them to protect them from their fears.

My career as a medical professional working in acute/palliative care was over; I could no longer perform my duties to assist those who needed my constant focus and total confidence. The constant anxiety of being in the hospital room began to show in my work ethic and in this field there is no room for error—when someone's life is at stake. I felt as though I was reliving the final

146

hours of Matthew's life every time I entered a patient's room. I would see him lying there, taking his last breath. I also tried to return to the clinic I had been at for a few years before and after Matthew's death, just to try and keep busy. I found that I no longer felt for the patients the way I had once. I could no longer tolerate the transients or drug addicts that would come in to seek medical attention. I would be angry with them, as I felt that perhaps their lifestyle choices were similar to those who had assaulted my son.

I also found myself becoming very upset when young men or women would come in after having been assaulted. I could no longer separate what was happening in my life with that of work. I have since not returned, and must try now to find other employment, and to think that once I thrived, and loved everything about my job, but now I must resort to trying to find something else.

I, unfortunately, will never trust again, I have a hatred for others that I never had before. I'm so very angry still, and this I have no doubt will take years to overcome. There are those who have asked me if I could ever find it in my heart to forgive the ones who did this, and I truly don't think I ever will. I pray that my son's face, and the sound of his screams haunt them for the rest of their living days, as I am haunted by these thoughts every moment of the day. I am plagued with night terrors, I can hear Matthew yelling for help, but I can't find him, I'm in a

147

panic, running, always running towards the sound of his voice, but I can't find him. I jolt from these night terrors, and cry uncontrollably, as the thought that my son is calling out for me to help him, and as a mother not being there to protect him when he needs me most, is a pain so great, I can physically feel it.

The financial strain that this has had on my family has been tremendous. I was ill-prepared for the cost of Matthew's funeral. I had no idea how we were going to come up with just under $30,000 in less than two weeks. A trust fund was set up, and had it not been for the kindness of strangers and family, my husband and I would not have been able to bury our son in a manner agreeable to our religious beliefs. It has taken my husband and I until now to finally pay back the financial institutions and our family members. The strain of this and my not returning to work has created unmentionable financial stress on my husband. He must now support me, and the three children on one income.

The toll this has taken on us can never be repaired. I think of all that Matthew would have grown to be, and all that he will never experience in life.

Matthew was to graduate from high school the following year, but instead, his chair was left empty, his name never called, to walk across the stage feeling triumphant. These things we will never have. Matthew will never know what it feels like to fall in love, to marry the girl of his dreams. He will never watch his own children come into this world. Matthew's life has been robbed of so many things that can never be replaced. Our lives will forever be altered, a life with so many dreams, and aspirations that will never come to fruition.

Not only has our family suffered this terrible loss, but we have had to endure in graphic details all that Matthew suffered that terrible night. The toll that the past few weeks of this trial has taken on our family is horrendous. Not only did we lose Matthew, but we also lost our father during the trial. My father died not even knowing the outcome of this trial. We must live the rest of our days, with the constant pain of what we have heard, and seen during this time. I can only pray that we will finally have some closure to this matter, and that my beautiful son will Rest in Peace."

—*Sandra Martins-Toner*

During my reading, Wendy poured me water, and handed me a box of tissues to wipe the tears from my eyes. I could hear sobbing throughout the courtroom, and was shocked to see that the reporters and sheriffs were also overcome by emotion. Pens scratched furiously across paper from the jury box, as the reporters tried to keep up. I looked over to Justice Romilly and he nodded his head and thanked me. I carefully and quickly walked back towards my family, hoping to be able to calm myself, and seek refuge in the comfort of their arms.

Chapter Twenty-Seven

SENTENCING AND JUDGE'S COMMENTS

Murder is unique in that it abolishes the party it injures,
so that society has to take the place of the victim and
on his behalf demand atonement or grant forgiveness;
it is the one crime in which society has a direct interest.

~ W. H. Auden ~

*W*e returned from the afternoon break feeling drained from the morning's emotional events. I found myself frustrated by the court's long, drawn-out procedures. I just wanted for the day to be over. A family member would take Chhaya out to play, so David and I could be together to hear the sentences handed down.

We all rose as Justice Romilly entered the courtroom. He began his oral decision by stating that the two accused, Robert Allan Forslund, and Katherine Anne Quinn were found guilty by a jury of second degree murder, on April 14th, 2007.

The jury had declined to make any recommendations with respect to the length of parole ineligibility. It was therefore up to the judge to make that determination.

Justice Romilly ordered that Forslund be sentenced to life imprisonment with no possibility of parole for a period of seventeen years. He then sentenced Quinn to life imprisonment, with no possibility of parole for a period of ten years. Our feelings were mixed on these sentences, as we felt Quinn could have received a longer ineligibility. Regardless of how long these two would sit in prison, nothing would ever bring my beautiful son back. It was I who had been handed a life sentence, as I would have to live the rest of my days without Matthew.

Justice Romilly then made some general comments, first citing the law and his role in sentencing. He explained the distinction between retribution and denunciation in sentencing, and then spoke directly to us.

"I wish to say something to the relatives of the deceased. I want you to understand that as a parent myself, I cannot help but feel your pain. I understand your anger at the accused for these vicious, brutal sadistic acts, this senseless killing. You must remember, however, that I operate within certain parameters. In imposing sentence I have to be faithful to the rule of law."

We understood from his comments that he truly empathized with us, and wished it were within his power to do more.

Justice Romilly then quoted from a judge's comment from another trial, "In my opinion the community is outraged by mindless violence, especially by mindless violence ending in death, and expects a killing to be expiated by a substantial term of imprisonment."

He concluded his decision by stating, "In my view, the circumstances reveal the murder of this young victim to have been senseless and brutal in the extreme. The death of the victim was lingering and painful. The courts have to send a message that this type of behaviour will not be tolerated, and that those who are convicted of this type of offence will receive little mercy from the courts. This type of brutal assault requires denunciation by society, deterrence of the accused and others from committing this type of offence and protection of the public."

The judge ordered, as a final part of the sentence, that a lifetime firearms ban be added to their conditions, and that both of the convicted provide a DNA sample to be held in a registry.

He further ordered that the time spent by the accused in custody would be considered "dead time," meaning that the time already spent in jail awaiting trial would not count towards their sentence. We were thrilled with this final touch, as the year spent in custody by Quinn prior to being granted bail, and the two years spent by Forslund, would not count as credit.

What many people are not aware of is that usually, time spent prior to a trial in a provincial facility is calculated at a double time rate, and subtracted from the length of the sentence. This means that a person who spent a year in jail waiting for trial would be granted two years off the sentence after trial. Justice Romilly had just ensured this couldn't happen with our case, forcing Quinn and Forslund to serve their entire time, from the date of sentencing.

We listened to the decision, letting it sink in and trying to process all that was said.

The sheriffs moved in to remove Forslund and Quinn from the prisoner's docks, and escorted them away to begin their sentences at a federal penitentiary. We all sat waiting or stood in the courtroom. We waited, wanting to see them being led away, wanting to witness their last walk as free citizens. We stifled an urge to applaud.

The crowd then disgorged into the hallway, everyone talking at once. Some praised the judge for a good job, and others complained that the sentences, Quinn's in particular, were not long enough.

We slowly made our way out of the courtroom, and out through the main doors, knowing that a press conference awaited us.

Wendy Dawson was being interviewed by the media. She was telling them Quinn was a person who would be a "danger in a dark alley or even on a lit street." Wendy also termed the brutality of the attack, "chilling and disturbing." She went on to say that, "The courts must protect safety on the streets and safety at SkyTrain stations."

Quinn's father told the media that he still believed in his daughter's innocence. Mr. Quinn also said, "Why wouldn't I? It's my daughter. She wasn't at the beating, nor was she at the crime scene when the attack occurred."

This statement by Mr. Quinn truly irritated me. I commented on this by stating that I felt they were in denial. The Quinns must remember that she had been convicted by twelve of her peers.

Forslund's lawyer, Karen Bastow, had nothing to say as the trial ended; she declined any comments.

Quinn's lawyer, James Millar, had not even cleared the main doors of the courthouse before he was already making comments to the media about filing an appeal. When the reporters asked him his grounds for such an appeal, he replied in vague terms, "a grossly unfair trial." He would not elaborate further. When we were asked about Millar's claims that he would be appealing the murder conviction, we simply stated that our family would be waiting and we were preparing ourselves. I then also told the reporters that this family was not going to back down. Millar was true to his word, although tardy. Court regulations stipulate that an accused has thirty days to apply for an appeal. Though he left it to the very end, he did manage to file his appeal application for Quinn on the 30th day after the sentence.

Chapter Twenty-Eight
POST-TRIAL LIFE—F.A.C.T. IS BORN

The only cure for grief is action.

~ George Henry Lewes ~

*I*t took us almost a week to return to a somewhat normal life after the trial, as we had just spent every single moment of the past few months consumed by the preliminary hearings, the *voir dire*, and the trial. Although we had found some consolation for the loss of our son, we couldn't get past the fact that he was never coming back.

I remember that at the end of the trial, after the sentences had been handed down, I was overcome with the feeling that Matthew would come running through the courtroom doors. I wanted my reward for having endured these past few years, and now I wanted my son back. Our children are supposed to bury us, not the other way around.

I needed to try to get my life back on track now that the trial was over. It would take some time to get used to being alone again with my thoughts, as I had spent so much time around others. I began to feel that my son was being forgotten, and all the other victims who had fallen prey to violent homicides began to take the spotlight in the local headlines.

Never again would I flip through the pages without reading about another family's loss. Never again would I simply say to myself, "Oh, those poor people." Instead I thought, "How can I reach out to them?"

I would never be the same person I was the day Matthew was murdered. I had been replaced by a much more aware woman, who would not stand by watching innocent victims and their families suffer in silence. I would not allow others to be re-victimized by our system.

It was at this time that I submerged myself in the organization I had founded with Nina Rivet. Throughout the course of the trial, I had stepped away from my obligations, but now I was ready to take on the criminal justice system. I wanted F.A.C.T. to become a household name. I wanted to build a solid foundation and to create a unified front by reaching out across Canada to other families like ourselves.

Due to the media exposure F.A.C.T. had begun to receive, we began to be contacted by others wanting our help. Nina began attending court with other families, and representing the group in the courthouses, while David assumed the public affairs position and dealt primarily with the media.

I created a brief that specifically addressed the lack of resources available under current government programs for victims and their families. The brief contained letters from families and detailed the re-victimization they had endured at the hands of the bureaucrats. More importantly, it offered practical solutions to satisfy the needs of crime victims.

This caught the attention of the Federal Ombudsman for Victims of Crime, a newly-created government position. The ombudsman was interested in meeting with us to discuss the issues. Steve Sullivan, a former director of the Canadian Resource Centre for Victims of Crime (CRCVC), met with us to discuss the lack of funding for victims programs. The meeting was, ironically, on what would have been Matthew's 18th birthday.

At the same time, we began receiving invitations from community service organizations, including the Rotary Clubs, to present at their meetings. David, wearing his public affairs hat, did the breakfast tour and made some valuable connections.

We began to see the strength of the networks we were establishing with the organization. Alone, I would have been nothing, a single voice in the wind. However, the combined strength of many with a common purpose was making headway. One family that became a critical part of the organization was the Penners. Gord and Kim had lost their son in much the same manner as we had, and we met for the first time at a Community Forum we held at the Friendship Gardens in New Westminster, B.C.

Gord quickly joined the group, and eventually became a F.A.C.T. board member. Gord and his family questioned why their own son's killer had been released on bail into the custody of a dysfunctional family. Ryan Crossley, their son's murderer, had already been convicted of violent crimes ten times and was a teen awaiting trial on yet another violent assault, when he killed Jesse. Gord and Kim demanded a public inquiry into the reasons why this violent youth had not been remanded into prison until his trial. Why had he been free to roam our streets?

It was at this time that a wonderful politician would take up Gord's fight, and F.A.C.T.'s cause. NDP MLA, Mike Farnworth, from the Port Coquitlam - Burke Mountain riding in B.C., would soon become an invaluable ally for the organization. Mike is the provincial Opposition House Leader, and serves as Opposition Critic for Public Safety and Solicitor General.

Mr. Farnworth and his assistant, Brad West, created and circulated a petition asking for the community to pressure the government into reviewing the reasons as to why Jesse's murderer was released into the community, and within days of the circulation, hundreds of signed petitions were returned from across Canada.

It was also Mr. Farnworth who took the time to sit with the F.A.C.T. Board of Directors to listen to our concerns. We addressed everything from the financial losses families endured after their loved one had been murdered, to creating and amending changes to the current laws and legislations pertaining to the (Y.C.J.A.), Youth Criminal Justice Act. Mike never disappointed us, and for this we have always been grateful.

Chapter Twenty-Nine
CHANGING THE LAW IN BRITISH COLUMBIA

Never forget that a small group of thoughtful people
could change the world.
Indeed, it's the only thing that ever has.

~ Margaret Mead ~

*I*n the spring of 2008, F.A.C.T. began drafting a Private Members' Bill to be introduced into the house. We had heard of too many cases like the Penners, or our own, where families had faced financial ruin over the death of a child.

Under existing Victim Services programs, the family of a child who is murdered isn't even considered a victim, and is therefore not eligible for many benefits, including wage loss.

We enlisted the help of Mr. Farnworth. We felt that if the current Liberal government in B.C. remained unresponsive to our pleas about this issue, then perhaps the official opposition might create some political pressure and public awareness.

Mike Farnworth worked very hard alongside our board of directors, and the finished draft, called Bill M-217: The Victims of Crime Compensation Act, was introduced in June, 2008.

Premier Gordon Campbell's Liberal Party had been conspicuously absent from any discussion on crime and victim's issues, although 2006 and 2007 were banner years from a crime standpoint.

There had been a record number of gangland killings, violent assaults, and even a mass murder in a Surrey condo complex. Crime seemed to elicit nothing more than stifled yawns from the Premier's office, and the odd innocuous sympathy newsbyte. No promises to change the existing policy—nothing to suggest any awakening or any official let's-get-tougher-on-crime platform. Zip. Nada. Nothing at all. We wondered what it would take to get this Premier's attention. We requested all of our F.A.C.T. supporters across the country to immediately write to their MLAs and Members of Parliament to request action on this issue and the speedy passage of helpful legislation. This mass e-mailing had the desired result, creating a ripple effect as thousands of concerned citizens bombarded government and other party representatives with letters. Within a week, our sources in government began to tell us our campaign had caused a real commotion. Our new bill, after passing first reading in the Legislature, needed a second reading to progress towards becoming law.

The Liberals didn't seem to know what to do. No doubt they were hesitant to openly support a Private Members' Bill that had been introduced by the Opposition. On the other hand, we had generated a huge amount of media interest with this bill, and to ignore it might not bode well for Campbell and his Liberals in the coming election.

We have always stressed that the issue of crime and public safety should be non-partisan. It transcends politics and party lines. We all want a safe world to raise our children in. I can't think of any legitimate reason that anyone, perhaps other than a defence lawyer, would not want their government to tackle the crime problem.

The spring session of the Legislature ended, with our bill still hanging, unfinished. We wondered if there would be a second reading when the Legislature reconvened.

In August of that year, there was a breakthrough. I had sent out a copy of Bill M-217 and letters to the Solicitor General of B.C. in regards to the Jesse Penner case. We asked the Solicitor General to formally review these issues. We were pleasantly surprised to receive a reply, requesting a meeting with the F.A.C.T. Board of Directors to address our concerns. The minister and several of his senior policy advisors sat with us for over two-and-a-half hours, reviewing the proposed bill and the Penners' concerns over the release of their son's killer.

It was an astounding day for me. For someone who had never been in a boardroom in her life, to be in a closed door meeting with senior government cabinet members was an accomplishment. What's

163

more, we came out of the meeting with some positive connections, and a commitment from the minister to work with us on our goals of improving services for victims of crime.

One week later, we ran into the minister again at a seminar for Victim Services workers, where we had been invited to present. He was so impressed with our presentation that he asked that copies be sent to him; he proceeded to distribute them to the entire caucus. I was later told by the director of the Crime Victims Assistance Program that she had received several copies of our PowerPoint presentation. It was obviously making the rounds.

We are currently meeting with senior Victim Services officials on a regular basis to try to amend the existing Crime Victim Assistance Act and push forward our own Private Members' Bill.

I have committed myself to working alongside the F.A.C.T. Board of Directors, our members and supporters to see that changes are made to improve the lot of crime victims. F.A.C.T. is willing to become the conduit through which the voices of our loved ones can be heard. We vow to never again be pushed aside, silenced or forgotten.

Chapter Thirty

A MOTHER'S MESSAGE TO HER SON'S KILLERS

*How much more grievous
are the consequences of anger
than the causes of it.*

~ Marcus Aurelius ~

I wanted to address my concerns that, throughout the trial, the media interviews, or any other public event, I have never been able to fully express myself regarding what happened that night. I have never really articulated the true impact that Matthew's murder has had on me.

As I mentioned earlier, family members aren't really looked upon as victims, but merely spectators, collateral damage to the offence. I knew that there were things that couldn't be said in the media, for fear of jeopardizing the trial. As a director of F.A.C.T., I had to be cautious not to express my personal opinions in a way that might reflect negatively on the organization. Most upsetting of all, I was restricted in what I could say in my victim impact statement, and had to adhere to the guidelines specified by the courts. It is unfortunate that even after we have found the accused guilty of the crime, we must continue to allow their rights to supersede those of the victims and their families. In our Canadian Charter of Rights it states the accused are "Innocent until Proven Guilty." In my opinion, it should be the other way around: "Guilty until Proven Innocent," at least for cases of murder, the most heinous crime that can be committed against another.

I know that I'm not at a point in my life where I could sit across from my son's killers, or even occupy the same room again. The pain is still too searing in my day-to-day life. I continue to struggle with the way in which my child's life was taken from him. I still replay that day in my head, wondering what I could have done to alter the course of it, what I could have said differently to Matthew that day to keep him from leaving the house. These things will haunt me forever, even though I know that I can't change what happened.

I have often imagined what I might say to my son's killers, had I the opportunity. I've also wondered what I might say to them if some day, by chance, this book fell into their laps while they sat in prison, serving their sentence for Matthew's murder.

I began thinking of the things I would say. Then I would talk myself out of it, telling myself that they are so hard-hearted and unreachable that they probably wouldn't care what I had to say anyway. Instead, I decided to write my most severe and anguished thoughts and place them in this book, on the slim chance that my written words would eventually reach them.

To the murderers who took my child's life,

It has been a little over three years now since you brutally and viciously took Matthew's life, and I want you to know that I will never forgive you for this. I don't know if, in your sick, twisted minds, you might imagine that you will someday find forgiveness, but it will not be from me.

There is not a day that goes by that I am not traumatized by the manner in which you did this. Matthew was the kindest, gentlest soul I have ever known, and the one person everyone could count on to be their friend. The emptiness you have caused in my life can never be replaced. You have taken away my best friend, my son, and a life so full of promise.

I keep wondering why you could not have just robbed him that night and left him to call me to come and get him. Why, why did you have to kill my baby? He was so little, and would never have had a chance against you. Matthew begged you for his life, but you continued to beat him to death. I remember holding his tiny hand in mine at the hospital and thinking to myself, what kind of monsters could have done this? He was kept draped under sheets and towels to protect us from seeing the damage you had done.

I had just told Matthew a few weeks before this happened that I was pregnant, and now he has a baby sister he will never be able to hold, watch grow, play with and love. Do you have any idea what you have done to this family, or how much pain you have caused us? I am plagued with visions of Matthew being beaten, begging for his life, but still you never stopped, you would continue to kill him.

I can only pray that Matthew will haunt you until the end of your days, and that every time you close your eyes, you will see the child you stole from me, and the child you left to die all alone on the cold pavement.

That night you not only broke Matthew, but you broke a piece of me. This was not an attack only on one boy, but on my entire family. You have left an empty spot at our table, a place that would have been filled by Matthew's laughter. The holidays and birthdays are no longer joyous events in our lives—instead, I dread them, because they are no longer the same without him.

As for you, Quinn, a mother of three children yourself, how could you murder another mother's child? I can only pray that your children will never suffer the way you made my little boy suffer. You can continue to lie to yourself, and your family, but we all know the truth.

You know the truth about what really happened that night. You know that the responsibility for what took place started with your actions, and instead of handing Forslund the bottle to finish Matthew, you could have stopped it.

You are the one person who could have calmed him and done the right thing, but instead you allowed it to continue. I hate you more than anything, more than anyone I've ever encountered. Your greed, pride, and arrogance have led you to where you are now, and I will do everything and anything in my power to keep you behind bars—where you belong.

I think you are a repugnant little pig for continuing to torment us with this ridiculous appeal, and I will pursue it to the Supreme Court of Canada if need be. I will never go away!

I will be present in sixteen years when Forslund is old and spent, the day he applies for parole. I will fight for the rest of my life to see that you never, ever hurt another innocent person again.

The courts may have given you life, a measly twenty-five years, but that is nothing in comparison to the life sentence you have given me without my beautiful son. I wasn't ready to say goodbye, but because of your actions, I am forced to live out the rest of my life without Matthew.

—Matthew Martins' Mom

Chapter Thirty-One

THE GROUP SPAWNED
BY MATT'S DEATH

There is never just one victim in a murder.
There's a chain-reaction of grief.

~ D.I. Rebus (author Ian Rankin) ~

Our lives have been altered so dramatically since that day, that none of us is anything like the person we once were. Everything we do is different. Even the friends we once had are no longer there. People don't know how to be around us anymore, or how to converse with us.

It's too hard for them to talk about all our old times together, since Matthew probably would have been with us. I think it has just made it easier for everyone to just avoid the inevitable awkwardness and move on, as hard as that may be. I miss our friends terribly, but I understand how it must be for them, as well.

Now, David and I and the others are running an organization for victims/families affected by violent crime, and have surrounded ourselves with others who are on the same page. We've been fortunate enough to make new friends, friends who have also lost children or a loved one to violent crimes. Through F.A.C.T. we met Gord and Kim Penner, a couple who have come to mean so very much to us and our children. The Penners also lost a beautiful son in a similar senseless and violent act. Jesse was murdered just months after our son, and this family suffered terribly as we had, so the understanding of one another's anguish was mirrored. We met a number of other families through F.A.C.T. and it's helped us in our journey.

Many people have asked me if working with F.A.C.T. has made it harder for me to heal, but the truth is, it has made it a little easier. We haven't allowed our loss to bury us. Instead, we have been tested by tragedy, and we discovered the beneficial change we could bring about. It gave us strength to be able to help others who have endured the same calamities. I vowed from the day Matthew was murdered to keep his memory alive, and if that meant telling his story for the rest of my days, I would.

I had to do something to keep his legacy alive, and in working with others in similar circumstances, I have been able to do just that. The issues that we have chosen to address will affect all those individuals and families who have been—or will be—touched by a violent crime.

I once thought Chhaya would be the only one not scarred by the terrible trauma. But I recognize now that she will live her entire life knowing she had a big brother, but never being able to hear his voice or his laughter or feel his hugs. She will never know the wonderful and beautiful person he was; the thought fills me with sorrow. I have been showing her pictures of Matthew from the moment she could sit up. Matthew's pictures are all over our house, including in her room; I never want a day to go by without looking at his beautiful face.

Chhaya says goodnight to him before bed as she passes his framed photo. The love that fills my heart at that very moment is indescribable.

I still visit his gravesite regularly and decorate his plot according to the holidays and seasons. It is the place I go to have a quiet moment with Matthew, and to read quietly to him. I feel at peace there, which is kind of ironic, since this will be my final resting place as well. When my time comes, Matthew and I will be reunited again. Our coffins will be placed one above the other, mother and child together again, forever and ever.

Epilogue
DAVID TONER ON CANADIAN JURISPRUDENCE

Injustice anywhere is a threat to justice everywhere.

~ Martin Luther King Jr. Letter from
Birmingham Jail, April 16, 1963 ~

*One who condones evils is just as guilty
as the one who perpetrates it.*

~ *Martin Luther King, Jr.* ~

*W*hen my wife asked me to write the epilogue for this book, I took
a considerable amount of time to decide how to approach it. Sandra
has done something that few others could, and has told the tragic
story of what happened to our son in a very raw, straightforward
and powerful way.

What is left to say? Perhaps just this—there are still many questions to be answered.

Three years after the death of my stepson, I am haunted by several questions. Not specifically questions related to his death, but ones that are broader, and perhaps much more difficult to answer:

- Why, in a country that is the envy of the world in many respects, are our own citizens so poorly represented and protected by those in authority?

- Why have the rights of the few—in this case, those accused of crimes, become so deeply entrenched in our legal system that they now supersede and render null the rights of the taxpaying citizens of this country?

- Why is justice so hard to find? I hesitate to even use the term "justice system" as anyone who has been victimized by a crime will attest to the fact that the criminal proceedings are far more concerned with the rights of the offender than those of the victim. What we really have is a "legal system," not a "justice system."

My fellow victims and I are not alone in this belief; a poll taken in the spring of 2008 found that a full 90% of those polled had no faith in the current Canadian criminal justice system.

How did things go so terribly wrong? The way I see it, the main pitfall of the system is this: *lack of responsibility.* This lack of responsibility is a social construct, beginning with the offenders, who are never required to take any responsibility for their actions.

This is especially true for young offenders, who are coddled by the Youth Criminal Justice Act, and held to a less stringent level of accountability, supposedly due to their inability to fully appreciate the consequences of their actions. Offenders of any age cannot be forced to testify, take part in programs or counselling, or participate in any rehabilitative training. Yet they enjoy the rights and freedoms guaranteed to all Canadians under the Charter.

The statutory release clause of the Criminal Code ensures that they don't even have to serve their full sentences for crimes committed, but are automatically freed after two-thirds of the sentence. At no point are they even required to admit their wrongdoing or take ownership of it.

The judiciary, too, are clearly exempt from any responsibility. I know of no other job where your performance is never questioned or reviewed, and there exists no mechanism for "debenching" a sitting judge, other than for gross personal misconduct. Judges can be lax, indifferent and even on some occasions, negligent in their duties and still face no repercussions, because the rule of "judicial independence" removes them from criticism or even basic accountability.

The government too, is to blame. Our government has abrogated their vaunted "social contract." There is an implicit duty on the part of the government to provide basic protection for the citizens of the country. These include: peace, order, and good government. These official requirements of the government are enshrined in the Preamble of the Canadian Constitution.

Private citizens long ago gave up their right to personally vindicate wrongs committed against them, in favour of allowing the state to exact justice on their behalf. It is a simple agreement, really. We no longer form lynch mobs to dole out street justice, and they keep order and protect the security of the nation. I would challenge anyone to say that the government has been satisfactorily holding up their end of the bargain in recent times. Social libertarian ideals have influenced legislators so that laws have been deliberately watered down. Rather than punish the guilty, in many cases legislation has magically made the transgression a non–crime. In many cases, our members of Parliament or MLAs have opted for rehabilitation over incarceration, even when the consequence is far greater risk to innocent parties.

You and I are the final players in this dance of irresponsibility. We, the people, have contributed to this fiasco, through our complacency and apathy.

"Fear not your enemies, for they can only kill you;
fear not your friends, for they can only betray you.
Fear only the indifferent,
who permit the killers and betrayers
to walk safely on the earth."

~Edward Yashinsky~

We have surrendered responsibility of our own safety and well–being. We have allowed those entrusted with running the justice system, including politicians, prosecutors, judges, Corrections Canada and the National Parole Board to conduct social experiments within that system, to the detriment and at the expense of innocent Canadian citizens.

Sandra Martins-Toner

We chose to ignore what was obviously a worsening situation through the 1980's and into the 1990's, as our law makers closed prisons and slashed the budgets of police forces. We sat there mute, then wondered why crime was rising. We stopped caring if our neighbour's car was stolen, as long as it was not ours. We looked the other way when we saw a fight in the street, because we didn't want to get involved.

We have become obsessed with studying the causes of crime, rather than dealing with it. Those who are "socially disadvantaged" make excuses for their crimes and blame their parents, the government, or the community for their woes. Everyone is responsible—anyone but themselves, of course.

Those of us who have been the victims of crime, or the survivors who have lost someone, can offer a very unique perspective on justice in this country. We have come to understand that social responsibility must be upheld and fought for.

After losing our son, we decided to make a difference. We found that because we spoke with a conviction and purpose few could imagine, people listened.

When my wife and I started Families Against Crime & Trauma, many took the view that it would be an advocacy group for the victims of crime, or a support group for the survivors of criminal acts. It has become both—and more. In taking on and criticising the government we have become a lobbyist organization, and a voice for those Canadians disenfranchised from the system. We have been careful to remain non-partisan, working with anyone and any party that shares our common goal. We will not cooperate with those who would use our tragedies as a platform for their own political agendas.

Several people suggested that F.A.C.T. should launch a political party of its own. However, we have found that we are freer to speak out about the shortcomings of the system if we aren't co-opted by the system. We don't care to become a part of it. The failing of any political party is that, regardless of their platform, they eventually become focused on perpetuating the party, rather than fulfilling their objectives.

F.A.C.T. serves a purpose that the government should address with vigour, but fails to. It bridges the gap between the victims of crime, and the participants in the justice system. The organization gives strength to those who have no voice, and our combined voices have a reach and an audience that any one of us alone would not have. We are not "revenge-driven, right-wing, hang-em-high," radicals. We are just concerned citizens who are trying to ensure the justice system is, indeed, "just." We have created a vehicle through which those who have been victimized, or those who are just aware and concerned, can exercise some social responsibility.

The answers I was seeking are found in the doing. We all have to do our part; we all have a role to play to make those guilty of crimes accountable, and to ensure that those who have the responsibility to administer the justice system do so in a responsible manner.

The question I now ask everyone I speak to is this: *What are YOU willing to do about it?*

David Toner
President of F.A.C.T.

ABOUT F.A.C.T.

Since we began F.A.C.T. a little over 3 years ago, we have gained National attention, and have established members/supporters across Canada.

We have gained credibility with the media, and are called upon regularly to speak out about the current state of our judiciary and comment on current cases before the courts.

F.A.C.T. has also begun to advocate on behalf of families who have been touched by violence.

We have built relationships with members of the Provincial & Federal Government in hopes of creating changes to the Criminal Code of Canada.

The need for support and guidance was not there for the families during their grievous time, so we decided to create an organization to help others.

We have become political allies for those in Parliament who believe in our cause, and a platform for victims/families to be heard. F.A.C.T. has caught the attention of the Provincial & Federal Government, Judiciary, Police Forces, legal Aide Services and the Communities.

We have been called by many a force to be reckoned with, and an organization to become involved with.

www.familiesagainstcrime.org

Appendix

MATTHEW—IN HIS OWN VOICE

*An essay written by Matthew at sixteen
for an English class*

Teen Parents

By: Matthew Martins

It wasn't until I started Kindergarten that I realized that my mom and dad weren't like the other parents. At first the clues were subtle, but as I observed the other parents that came to pick up my classmates after school, I knew something was definitely different. This difference was that my mom and dad were younger, I mean much younger than the other parents. I didn't really know when I asked my mom why they all looked so much older, until later in my life.

My mom was only 16 when she found out that she was pregnant with me, and my dad was 18. My mom was asked to leave her high school, as the school felt that she was a bad influence on the other kids at school. She remained at home with her mom and dad until after I was born, so that my grandma could help her take care of me.

I was born on September 20, 1988 and my mom had just turned 17. My mom has always told me that I was meant to be, and that she would never change a thing, but she has made it clear as I grew older, that she would never want for any teen to have to face such responsibility, especially me.

I have watched my mom finish high school and work crappy jobs. My mom eventually married my dad when I was 3 years old. My dad wasn't a very good father or husband. My mom had two more kids, my little brothers. It wasn't until the youngest was born that my mom couldn't take the physical and emotional abuse from my dad anymore. When my youngest brother was only 6 months old, my mom packed it up. It would honestly take far too long to explain what we went through at this point in my life, but let's just say it was hard for all of us.

The one significant thing that I learned at this time was that what does not kill you will make you stronger. I resented both my parents for a very long time. I acted out in various forms to try and get back at them. All I wanted was some damn normalcy in my life.

A few years later my mom met my step-dad. This was really odd at first, but you know what—he listened when I spoke; he took the time to really get to know me and my siblings. My biological father has only recently begun to see me again. It's different though, we're like friends. My little brothers don't even know him.

It's really sad that any guy can be a father or sperm donor per say, but it takes a real man to be a father. Through all this my mom and I have grown up together, really. We have a great relationship and an understanding of each other. I'm so proud of my mom as she has recently graduated from University with an excellent grade point average. She now has a great job working in a hospital, doing what she loves, and that's taking care of others.

Now that I am 16, I couldn't imagine being a parent. I honestly don't think I would know the first thing about it. I have learnt so much from my mom, especially to strive for better and to never give up.

The personal experience that I have shared with you is that you have to be responsible for all your actions in life. I also learned that your parents don't have to be blood, they just have to be parents.

Editor – David Yanor

This book would not be complete without extending a very special thanks to my Editor, David Yanor. I truly feel that he was sent my way through a heavenly whisper. David allowed my voice to carry throughout the book, and ensured that no page was left unturned.

I am very pleased with David's incisive observations and perceptive edits. He's a talented wordsmith and a dedicated professional.

To have been able to find an editor who has also lost a loved one to a violent act, and who understood first hand the pain a family endures is not coincidental, but fate. You were instrumental in helping me find my voice, and your excellence for fine details is unsurpassable. Your honesty, compassion and praise made this experience one I will never forget. I know that we will work together in all my future endeavours.

—Sandra Martins-Toner